Cawdor

Medea

Robinson Jeffers

A LONG POEM *Cawdor*

Medea AFTER EURIPIDES

A NEW DIRECTIONS BOOK

Library of Congress Catalog Card Number: 76-103374

ACKNOWLEDGMENT: Two passages from *Cawdor*, "The Old Man's Dream after He Died" and "The Caged Eagle's Death Dream" are reprinted from *The Selected Poetry of Robinson Jeffers* by permission of Random House, Inc.

Cawdor was first published by Random House in 1928.
Medea was first published by Random House in 1946.

First published as ND Paperbook 293 in 1970
Published simultaneously in Canada by Penguin Books Canada Limited.
Manufactured in the United States of America
New Directions books are printed on acid-free paper

New Directions Books are published for James Laughlin
by New Directions Publishing Corporation,
80 Eighth Avenue, New York 10011

NINTH PRINTING

Contents

INTRODUCTION by William Everson (Brother Antoninus)   vii

Cawdor   3

Medea   113

Introduction

By William Everson (Brother Antoninus)
Author of *Robinson Jeffers: Fragments of an Older Fury*

I

This book places in the hands of a new generation of readers two of the long, somber and God-tormented poems of Robinson Jeffers. The first, the verse narrative *Cawdor*, is laid in the Big Sur on the California coast, the locale Jeffers knew thoroughly and used repeatedly to body forth his misgivings about the human race. The other, a redaction of the *Medea* of Euripides, is a free adaptation from the Greek written for the stage. *Cawdor* appeared in 1928 at the height of Jeffers' career, and was enthusiastically received. It is a superb example of his outlook and narrative method. *Medea*, published in 1946, was written specially for the actress Judith Anderson. The combined genius of poet and tragedienne proved irresistible when the play was staged the following year, and it is remembered as the outstanding success of its period. Both poems have long been out of print.

The current preoccupation with mysticism, everywhere evident in the verse now being written, will gain sustenance from this reintroduction to one of the most powerfully visionary poets that America has produced. Only Whitman rivals him in this regard, though Whitman's greater universality is rather more ethical than religious; despite his range he displays nothing like the terrible intensity of Jeffers' religious passion. Nevertheless each poet presents a distinct facet of what might be called our fundamental native pantheism:[1] by the singularity of his achievement each complements the other. They define between them the positive and negative poles of the unconscious American religious spirit.

Cawdor tells what can happen when a widower past his prime, unable to relinquish youth, marries a nubile girl. It was a theme founded in Jeffers' bloodstream, for he was himself the progeny of such a union. His father, no widower indeed but a frosty Presbyterian minister, took late in life an attractive young bride. Born in 1887 in Pittsburgh, Jeffers' childhood was lonely. He was educated there and at various private schools in Europe until his parents moved to Pasadena where he entered Occidental College. Doing his advanced study in science at the University of Southern California he graduated with honors but determined to become a poet. True to his oedipal background he wooed the beautiful wife of a socially prominent Los Angeles lawyer, and when he had won her carried her off to the magnificent isolation of the Monterey coast. This was in 1914. He built there a stone tower and began the remote life that was to become legendary. His first two volumes of verse were not significant, but in 1924 he made his breakthrough with a privately published narrative poem, *Tamar*, which became an overnight sensation. It was evident that the latent American pantheistic seed had found its Californian fertility,[2] and a new breed was born. But it was not destined for tranquility: from that time on, though his productivity never abated, Jeffers' career was stormy. His verse fought with the times. After World War II the nation turned its back on him, the Eisenhower era being especially unsympathetic, and at his death he was no longer widely read. As Frederic I. Carpenter was to write in summation:

> Considered historically, Jeffers remains one of the most important poets of the years before the great depression. But in the last quarter of a century his reputation has fluctuated not only with the events and tastes of the times but with the changing tone and quality of his own successive poems. Always a few readers—including some major poets and critics—have con-

sidered his work of the greatest permanent value. Always
other readers—including many major critics—have considered
it beneath notice. Few authors in the history of literature have
excited greater differences of opinion; and few have seen their
reputations change so greatly in their own lifetimes. But
critical praise and blame affected Jeffers himself very little.
From his isolated rock tower he continued to gaze southward
at the wild promontories of the coast and westward at the far
horizons of the ocean, rather than eastward at his fellow men.[3]

But the times come round. An economy of affluence and a mangling
Viet Nam war have conspired to prepare an atmosphere of dis-
enchantment and risk not unlike the mood in which Jeffers himself
had quickened. Perhaps a new generation, sick of the suburbs, is
finding his Big Sur isolation and his westering gaze as universal in
their implications as an intermediate generation found them
irrelevant.[4]

II

A great deal has been written about the philosophical background of
Jeffers' thought in Lucretius, Nietzsche and Spengler. However, the
best way to get him in focus is as a native transcendentalist—but, it
must be remembered, a transcendentalist gone West and turned
inside out. As with Whitman, Emerson shaped his mind. One of the
first of his recently published letters lets us see him as the ardent
young poet writing to his girl: "As you remarked, most beautiful,
Emerson's a great and good man. We've had only two great men yet
in American literature—Poe is the other."[5] And years later, in his
creative maturity, answering a query from Carpenter, he could say:
"Emerson was a youthful enthusiasm, if you like, but not outgrown
by any means, only read so thoroughly that I have not returned to
him for a long time."[6]

Actually, it was Emerson's prose more than any other element
that formed the ground for Jeffers' meditative poetic style. Jeffers

emerged at the height of the Modernist triumph, but of its aesthetic tenets he utilized only one, the one that transformed him from a minor to a major artist. Against the Georgians, who looked back to the Romantics, the Modernists insisted that poetry must assimilate the techniques developed in the refinement of contemporary prose style. It was the chief break with the past that brought poetry up to date. Jeffers followed suit, and presented the resilient, massive, intellectually resonant verse idiom that enabled him to assail with such authority the complacencies of his time. When someone gets around to it, following out the implications of this particular Modernist tenet, and makes a study of the prose stylists who stand behind the major modern poets, it will be plain that for Jeffers the matrix was Emerson. Time and again his sonorous diction haunts the Jeffersian line:

> But man is conscious,
> He brings the world to focus in a feeling brain,
> In a net of nerves catches the splendor of things,
> Breaks the somnambulism of nature . . .[7]

What turned Jeffers' youthful transcendentalism inside out was World War I, the single most disillusioning event in our national history. Jeffers emerged from it with his idealism shattered. Under the shadow of ten million slain all the benignancy of Victorian optimism turned to dust and ashes in the mouths of thousands, and if Hemingway became their spokesman, Jeffers became their prophet. Just as he took the positive element in his father's religion and reversed it against itself, so he took the confident element in his master, and controverted it through the menstrum of his wary disenchantment. Thus what Emerson saw for a wonder:

> There is something social and intrusive in the nature of all things; they seek to penetrate and overpower each the nature of every other creature, and itself alone in all modes and throughout space and spirit to prevail and possess. Every star in heaven is discontented and insatiable . . .[8]

Jeffers saw for a curse:

> You would be wise, you far stars,
> To flee with the speed of light this infection.
> For here the good sane invulnerable material
> And nature of things more and more grows alive and cries.
> The rock and water grow human, the bitter weed
> Of consciousness catches the sun, it clings to the near stars,
> Even the nearer portion of the universal God
> Seems to become conscious, yearns and rejoices
> And suffers: I believe this hurt will be healed
> Some age of time after mankind has died,
> Then the sun will say "What ailed me a moment?" and resume
> The old soulless triumph, and the iron and stone earth
> With confident inorganic glory obliterate
> Her ruins and fossils . . .[9]

Or what Emerson, in a marvelous passage from the same essay, could rejoice in:

> A man should know himself for a necessary actor. A link was
> wanting between two craving parts of nature, and he was hurled
> into being as the bridge over that yawning need, the medi-
> ator betwixt two else unmarriagable facts. His two parents
> held each of them one of the wants, and the union of foreign
> constitutions in him enables him to do gladly and gracefully
> what the assembled human race could not have sufficed to
> do . . . The thoughts he delights to utter are the reason of his
> incarnation . . . Hereto was he born, to deliver the thought of
> his heart from the universe to the universe; to do an office which
> nature could not forego, nor he be discharged from rendering,
> and then immerge again into the holy silence and eternity out
> of which as a man he arose . . .[10]

This becomes, for Jeffers, in an equally marvelous passage from his same poem, a concurrence indeed but also a demur:

> And have widened in my idleness
> The disastrous personality of life with poems,
> That are pleasant enough in the breeding but go bitterly at last

To envy oblivion and the early deaths of nobler
Verse, and much nobler flesh;
And I have projected my spirit
Behind the superb sufficient forehead of nature
To gift the inhuman God with this rankling consciousness.

But who is our judge? It is likely the enormous
Beauty of the world requires for completion our ghostly
        increment,
It has to dream, and dream badly, a moment of its night.[11]

In his roots, then, Jeffers retained the grandeur and scale of the transcendentalist vision, even as this quotation makes evident, regardless how deceptive his negativism appeared to those looking for sources. What they saw was that he stood as polar opposite to Whitman, and this is true enough; but of itself the fact does not establish him a nihilist.

Whitman was of the balloon age; he lived in the high atmosphere of sun and wind and bouyant clouds. Jeffers, however, broke through the stratosphere: he looked back at the earth from the blackness of outer space. Writing in 1923, when aircraft were capable of no more than a couple hundred miles an hour in a dive, he could prophecy:

Far flown ones, you children of the hawk's dream future,
    when you lean from a crag of the last planet on the ocean
Of the far stars, remember we also have known beauty.[12]

In this, for once, he was justified in his own life. If he was not to be here to see the moon-landings, at least he was present for the space-advent of Yuri Gargarin.

III

The thing that conceals Jeffers' transcendentalism is its extremity; it is so extreme that humanity is dwarfed, reduced by the cosmic vision that has carried the poet out beyond the range of the human dimension, and gives him the eyes of God. Whitman has been called an arch-transcendentalist,[13] and indeed he is, but that leaves no term for Jeffers. Jeffers pushes the tenets of the creed beyond the point of no return. He crossed that line with his first major poem, *Tamar*, and from the breakthrough-position that it established for him there was no turning back. It is true that all his poems were to be involved with the life of man on earth, but that life is seen from another dimension. It is very like the gaze of an adult grown wise looking back upon a disgustingly precocious childhood.

Once Jeffers made his breakthrough he was compelled to extend its implications, and he wrote like a man possessed. After *Tamar* there followed in rapid succession "The Tower Beyond Tragedy" and *Roan Stallion* in 1926, and then, apocalyptically, *The Women at Point Sur* in 1927, where the last mask was torn from the human face as he saw it. But "*Tamar* seemed to my later thought," he was to write in explanation, "to have a tendency to romanticise unmoral freedom, and it was evident a good many people took it that way. . . one of my later intentions of the *Point Sur* was to indicate the destruction and strip everything but its natural ugliness from the unmorality."[14] There were other intentions, certainly, and their aptness is disputed, but as to this one there can be no dispute. However much the purgative of *Point Sur* relieved *him* his readers were, almost to a man, revolted. He realized that its extremity had placed in jeopardy his deeper message.

This brings us to the first of the paired poems which comprise this book, for it is with *Cawdor* that he attempted to mend his fences. His aim was to write a simple narrative, classically sound, in which his doctrine, his "Inhumanism," as he was to call it, is implicit, not obtrusive. It is, therefore, more than any other of his long poems, a "straight narrative," one with fewer allegorical overtones. Perhaps, prophet that he was, and no "teller of tales to delight women and the people,"[15] this is the real reason why he excluded it from his *Selected Poetry* when he came to compile that impressive volume nine years later.

The main point, however, is that his stratagem was successful.

Cawdor, published the year after *Point Sur*, righted the yawing course of his career and has been widely praised. Of it Lawrence Clark Powell, the poet's first major commentator, was to say:

> This is, in my opinion, Jeffers' finest single volume: the verse in it is on a consistently high level. Whereas some of the narratives in the *Roan Stallion* volume are overburdened with doctrine, and *The Women at Point Sur* is loud with the horns of prophecy, *Cawdor* is a tale told for the telling; and though very serious in tone and marked by awful, violent acts, it is free from themes of incest and sexual perversion. Unlike the mad minister of *The Women at Point Sur*, the protagonist Cawdor is consistently sane. His tragedy, which proceeds inevitably from the postulates, is not one of abnormality, and hence is more likely to be appreciated by the general reader.[16]

Even Yvor Winters, Jeffers' most savagely hostile critic, found good in it. "*Cawdor* alone of Mr. Jeffers' poems contains a plot that in its rough outlines might be sound, and *Cawdor* likewise contains his best poetry; the poem as a whole, and in spite of the confused treatment of the woman, is moving, and the lines describing the seals at dawn are fine, as are the two or three last lines of the apotheosis of the eagle . . ."[17]

But for all Jeffers' resolution to write a straight narrative there are focal points within it from which his transcendental proclivities refuse to be excluded. These are the deaths. The first two, those of Old Frazer and the youth Hood Cawdor, are seen as disintegrative and deliquescent. They represent diffuse human consciousness incapable of achieving sufficient concentration to survive after life. The final death, that of the eagle, is integrative and transcendent. Counteracting the human weaknesses, it indicts them with an upward rush, soars into the realm of the super-real. The eagle, ancient symbol of height, of the spirit as the sun, and of the spiritual principle in general, serves powerfully to liberate Jeffers' mystical imagination. Its deathflight is one of the matchless examples of the transcendental intuition in English.

The descriptive processes shown in the human deaths have also impressed readers but they have not been so well understood symbolically. They might be called further instances of what Hyatt H. Waggoner rebukes as "the dubious taste of writing about a man by talking about the electrons and molecules that are supposed to account for him."[18] Jeffers, rather, is taking these deaths, eagle and man, as polar opposites, and using them symbolically to define the nature of the consequence that inheres in each. He is taking both the disintegrative ego-centric death of man and the trans-egoistic death of the eagle as instances in an inferred teleological ultimacy.

To Jeffers the eagle is more "real" than the man because it symbolizes a type of consciousness that is not divided within itself. It has not mis-evolved into an offshoot or sport of ratiocination as has that of man. A Catholic would say that while he sees human nature as "fallen" he sees that of the eagle as "angelic." Like an angel the eagle for Jeffers is more point-focused within its intrinsic nature, more "all there" as we would say, because it is not self-preoccupied in the flawed and divisive human way. In scholastic angelology a well-known impromptu definition has it that an angel is "a thinking thought." For Jeffers an eagle is "an acting act," and in rendering its death he evaporates language in an effort to register the intensity of his intuition. To those critics who protest that an eagle is not an angel I do not know how to reply, unable at this remove to argue the matter of how one reads poetry. At any rate it is good theology to infer that we become after death pretty much what we have made of ourselves in this life, and Jeffers reduces human desire to its normative processes in civilized life and projects from these its metaphysical consequences. Looking at man he sees in his death-act the ultimate atomization of consciousness that life had only served to accelerate in him. One way of expressing this is to particularize the disintegrating electrons and molecules of his being in physical decomposition, whether or not they really are "supposed to account for him." However that may be, the description of this process in Cawdor is, as Powell had observed, "unique in literature."

The case of Medea is more complex and more difficult to discuss, bringing as it does into sharper focus than *Cawdor* the whole matter of Jeffers' relation to the tragic tradition in literature. In the matter of form the two poems share a common feature. Though one is narrative and the other dramatic, though one is "modern" and the other "classical," neither originated in the deeps of his creative unconscious; both were tailored to exterior requirements. *Cawdor* was composed to the situation following *Point Sur*; in the case of *Medea* the poet was approached by a theatrical producer. This objectivity gives them greater formal restraint; they are more Apollonian than the characteristically Dionysian pieces of Jeffers' creative unconscious. "Only his adaption of the *Medea*," writes Radcliffe Squires, "realizes Jeffers' own aim in tragedy as 'poetry . . . beautiful shapes . . . violence.' And this only because of the organic simplicity that Euripides imposes on Jeffers' restive imagination."[19] The reader of the present book, therefore, will see Jeffers "at his best" from the formal point of view. But if he wishes to touch the nerve of the master he will have to follow him into darker regions of his labyrinthine soul.[20] Squires concludes:

> Almost everywhere else in Jeffers' poetry the contentions grind against each other, reducing human character to dust, destroying those very structures and relationships which recommend themselves as essential to narrative and dramatic success. I cheerfully concede these points to Jeffers' detractors. Nor do I wish to minimize these faults. Yet even after such a large loss, something larger remains, and if we do not minimize this remainder, we see that it is poetry.

IV

As for Jeffers' relation to the tragic tradition in literature, he himself spoke of it as functional: "An exhibition of essential elements by the burning away through pain and ruin of inertia and the unessential." Rudolf Gilbert describes the process this way: "What to Athanasius was divinity, to Jeffers is nature—nature and divinity always separated from humanity. It is when the natural in humanity is crushed out by materialism that evil enters and tragedy begins."[21] This, however, is not really the issue as it emerges from the deepest reading of Jeffers' poems.

In order to clarify, let us set Jeffers' practice against the continuity of the tragic as it evolved in human consciousness. Emerson writes:

> The bitterest tragic element in life to be derived from an intellectual source is the belief in a brute Fate or Destiny; the belief that the order of Nature and events is controlled by a law not adapted to man, nor man to that, but which holds on its way to the end, serving him if his wishes chance to lie in the same course, crushing him if his wishes lie contrary to it, and heedless whether it serves or crushes him. This is the terrible meaning that lies at the foundation of the old Greek tragedy, and makes the Oedipus and Antigone and Orestes objects of such hopeless commiseration. They must perish, and there is no overgod to stop or mollify this hideous enginery that grinds or thunders, and snatches them up into its terriffic system.[22]

Jeffers sometimes draws on this tradition but not to serve this reason, and certainly not in *Cawdor*. Here disaster springs from the manifest sexual vanity that leads its protagonist to wive a girl he knows does not love him, representing a kind of karmic fulfillment that, thought not lacking in inevitability, is not tragic in the above sense. The narrative, as Powell says, "proceeds from its postulates." But while karmic outworking can be recognized in the tragedies of Jeffers, as it is here, it is never his message. It is not the reason he writes.

Returning to the "classic" situation as Emerson describes it above, we must insist that, regardless how many instances occur in Jeffers' narratives which seem to verify this viewpoint—blind, mindless butcherings and catastrophes—it is not the basic Jeffersian thesis. Nor can it be ever again for man, and Emerson shows why:

> But this terror of contravening an unascertained and unascertainable will cannot co-exist with reflection: it disappears

with civilization, and can no more be reproduced than the fear of ghosts in childhood. It is discriminated from the doctrine of Philosophical Necessity herein: that the last is an Optimism, and therefore the suffering individual finds his good consulted in the good of all, of which he is a part. But in destiny, it is not the good of the whole or the *best will* that is enacted, but only *one particular will*. Destiny properly is not a will at all, but an immense whim; and this is the only ground of terror and despair in the rational mind, and of tragedy in literature. Hence the antique tragedy which was founded on this faith, can never be reproduced.[23]

Because this is so, Jeffers' redactions of the Greek tragedies have often been unthinkingly dismissed as falsifications, rendered "morally and emotionally meaningless," in the words of Winters, by the differing conclusions to which he was constrained to direct them. Here we see the poet wiser than his critics. Emerson continues:

After reason and faith have introduced a better public and private tradition, the tragic element is somewhat circumscribed. There must always remain, however, the hindrance of our private satisfaction by the laws of the world. The law which establishes nature and the human race, continually thwarts the will of ignorant individuals, and this in the particulars of disease, want, insecurity and disunion.[24]

This of course is the situation of the man Cawdor, and we are wont to call it tragic, but Emerson distinguishes:

But the essence of tragedy does not seem to me to lie in any list of particular evils. After we have enumerated famine, fever, inaptitude, mutilation, rack, madness and loss of friends, we have not yet included the proper tragic element, which is Terror, and which does not respect definite evils but indefinite; an ominous spirit which haunts the afternoon and night, idleness and solitude.[25]

It is at this point that we meet the situation of *Medea*, and it compels Jeffers to the most extraordinary devices to accomodate its *dénouement* to such a view of reality and human destiny. The cloak that destroys Medea's rival is straight out of Euripides, of course, but Jeffers' employment of archetypal fire-serpents to protect her at the play's close is an acknowledged improvement upon the Euripidean device of openly driving her off in a chariot. They seem to canalize the Terror and give it concreteness in the poet's abrasive onslaught on human egoism. But there still remains the high registration of Jeffers' tragic spirit in an area that Emerson does not consider.

For at this point Jeffers parts company with his master, who now begins to subjectivize the problem of the tragic, and for its solution turns another way:

> A low haggard sprite sits by our side, "casting the fashion of uncertain evils"—a sinister presentiment, a power of the imagination to dislocate things orderly and cheerful and show them in startling array ... And accordingly it is natures not clear, not of quick and steady perceptions, but imperfect characters from which somewhat is hidden that all others see, who suffer most from these causes. In these persons who move the profoundest pity, tragedy seems to consist in a temperament, not in events. There are people who have an appetite for grief, pleasure is not strong enough and they crave pain, mithridatic stomachs which must be fed on poisoned bread, natures so doomed that no prosperity can soothe their ragged and dishevelled desolation. They mis-hear and mis-behold, they suspect and dread. They handle every nettle and ivy in the hedge, and tread on every snake in the meadow.[26]

So pronounced is Jeffers' penchant for anguish and catastrophe that the convinced Emersonian might well be tempted to dismiss his preoccupation as no more than this. Truly, if any modern writer can be so described, Jeffers has a "mithridatic stomach." But while subjectivity might explain the emotional coloring of a tragedian it says nothing about his metaphysical assumptions or his aesthetic resolutions.

No, with Jeffers we have to go to the religious solution. He shares with the Christian both a refusal to dismiss the evils of the world and a search for an answer to tragedy in the doctrine of salvation. In this he is more traditional than Emerson, holding to an insight memorialized in all the great religions of the world. Emerson's solution is unquestionably courageous. By subjectivizing its impress ("Tragedy is in the eye of the beholder") he looks within the interplay of forces for the compensatory reaction which will correct the excess that produced the fatality. In the end he seeks for the answer in the interior life alone:

> The intellect is a consolor, which delights in detaching or putting an interval between a man and his fortune, and so converts the sufferer into a spectator and his pain into poetry. It yields the joys of conversation, of letters and of science. Hence also the torments of life become tuneful tragedy, solemn and soft with music, and garnished with rich dark pictures. But higher still than the activities of art, the intellect in its purity and the moral sense in its purity are not distinquished from each other, and both ravish us into a region whereunto these passionate clouds of sorrow cannot rise.[27]

This is indeed what might be called the modern interpretation of the ancient tragic problem. Joseph Wood Krutch writes of it as "a profession of faith, and a sort of a religion; a way of looking at life by virtue of which it is robbed of its pain. The sturdy soul of the tragic author seizes upon suffering and uses it only as a means by which joy may be wrung out of existence."[28] But this is not Jeffers. No author who ever lived was less interested in converting pain into pleasure than he.

V

For Emerson's mind was primarily philosophic, as of course is that of Krutch, while Jeffers was essentially religious, and in the most primitive and elemental sense: it is this alone that wrenched him from the beneficent solutions of the sage of Concord. Ineradicable in his consciousness is the doctrine of Original Sin. He cannot posit a "fall," with its direct moral imputations, but he does posit a past evolutionary mishap. The moral imputation enters through man's wilful adhering to his inherited liabilities in preference to ontological existence as evidenced in prime nature. Jeffers discerns, empirically enough, man's alienation from reality, and what matter if he attribute it to an evolutionary fluke, a biological mischance in the geneaology of the species? The operative point is that the evils he delineates in his narratives stem from a human penchant which is not hypothetical. As with the Christian, "salvation" lies in deliverance, and though deliverance for him amounts to assimilation into the cosmos, that cosmos is not, essentially, material. What we die into is God. Jeffers supports his torrential violence and redeems his tragedies, as do the major Christian poets, by suffusing creation—action and context alike—with a God-presence that assimilates the anguish of victims into a more intense dimension. By every poetic device at his command he sustains an elevation above the catastrophe he so graphically delineates. It is the technique of the author of Job, employing mood, imagery, rhythm, metaphor—device after device—to proclaim the God-consciousness he knows is sustaining the cruelty and which constitutes its meaning. Of these the most powerful weapon is mood, his incredible atmospherics. Despite the many faults and contradictions assailed by critics it can be fairly argued that he fails only when he fails in this.

> If complete unity of structure seems to be lacking in the narratives, unity of mood and atmosphere does not. Here Jeffers is a master. From the first to the last lines we are immersed in a tragic world, dream-laden with violence and anguish. As Dostoievski depicts a gray Russian world, Jeffers draws his with blood-images against fogs and treacherous promontories ... The background of raging nature, together with the distorted lives of the characters, merge in turbulent images. All are underscored by the heavy, sometimes ponderous meter that supplies the muffled rhythm. Few readers of Jeffers can forget the oppressive mood he generates. It is a mood of black romanticism which brings into focus the doctrine as well as the

dourness of tone, and we may be convinced, as Jeffers wants us to be, that life needs a reevaluation if things are really so bad. Through this depressing convergence of image, setting, subject and tone, Jeffers comes closest to achieving his purpose, and we begin to believe that "We must uncenter our minds from ourselves" to escape catastrophe.[29]

Thus he uses pain, as does the Christian poet, as the primary separating agent between the ego-centric human consciousness and a super-reality which heightens the pain even as it dwarfs it. This dwarfing through intensification is what the martyrs of all religious faiths have experienced time and again, and Jeffers is its great modern literary advocate. It is through his suffering that man may see God. Thus the heaping on of violence in Jeffers is proportioned to our sensual insularity, for which our multiple soporifics have rendered pain innocuous. He scours the encrustations of civilization from the nerves of his characters not so that they might know joy, but so that we, his readers, might recognize God, and die.

I observed above that in *Medea* Jeffers drew upon the aspect of the tragic that Emerson localized in the heart of unmitigated Terror. In this he followed Euripides, and said no more. If in doing so a certain organic simplicity of form was imposed on Jeffers' restive imagination, as Squires has indicated, it is done at the cost of what he himself had to say about it. For in *Solstice*, his earlier adaptation of the play to narrative verse, where no such restriction inhibited him, the deep probe of his insight is more apparent, and though it is thought to be the worst poem he ever wrote[30] his informing conviction is unmistakable. Nor can this be dismissed as one more instance of the twisting of classic themes in order to further personal ends, for even in Euripides something more is implied. In his *Greek Tragedy* H. D. F. Kitto writes:

> But if we look carefully into the last scene we shall see more than dramatic convenience in the chariot. Medea has done things which appal even the chorus, those sympathetic neighbours who had said, earlier in the play, "Now is honor come to womankind." Their prayer now is "O Earth, O thou blazing light of

the sun, look upon this accursed woman before she slays her own children ... O god-given light, stay her hand, frustrate her ..." In the same vein Jason says, when he has learnt the worst, "After doing this, of all things most unholy, dost thou show thy face to the Sun and the Earth?" Sun and earth, the most elemental things in the universe, have been outraged by these terrible crimes; what will they do? how will they avenge their sullied purity? What Earth will do we shall not be told, but we are told what the Sun does: he sends a chariot to rescue the murderess.[31]

Why? In *Solstice* Jeffers spells it out. His primitive religious intuition drives back behind the Euripidean implication to what must have been the deeper mythical source of this legend. He recognizes that what is at stake, what is at war in the soul of Medea, is the ineluctable contest between the Sacred and the Profane. This inexorable tension carries her beyond a human struggle between jealous rage and maternal devotion which, by Euripides' time, had for the sophisticated Greek consciousness become a point of burning concern. Rather it is a demonstration of the authority and triumph of the Sacred, and it proclaims to mankind that so crucial is this opposition that when human lives enter its arena they must be prepared to encounter the fundamental cleavage in reality. Medea is a woman in whom the archetype of the Sacred is so primitive and unadulterated that it will not permit her to accept the accommodations of normative life. Rather she is invaded by the sacral and compelled to follow its directive, which declares that children are better dead than corrupt. This is, of course, the basic Jeffersian attitude, but in this play he utilizes the dimension of Terror to render it shockingly plain.

From this it can be seen that Jeffers' solution to the problem of the tragic is essentially salvivic, and that the mode of salvation is faith. Medea is saved through the capacity of the human spirit to adhere to a principle beyond itself, and by abnegation and transcendence achieve identity with that principle; to qualify for its attributes by accepting subsumption into it, even to the ultimate nullification of the individual identity, as happens to Madrone

Bothwell in *Solstice* if not to Medea. Jeffers is not a gnostic in that he offers no technique by which the elect, the spiritual cognoscenti, may effect transcendence, and so escape the trap of material contingency. And he is not a Christian in that he repudiates incarnation as a synthesis between the opposed polarities of matter and spirit: the Word made Flesh.

For Jeffers, existence offers, through consciousness, one redeeming aspect: the instant of recognition, one moment in which to behold the real, and then suffer its invasion. This is not so good as the hawks, who *act* the real in a way we can't; or the rocks, who *concretize* it in a way we can't; but it is all we have. To refuse it, to pervert consciousness into self-congratulatory preening of the collective ego, is to miss the sublime opportunity of all evolution. To refuse is to fail. But to accept its moment of anguish and catastrophe is, as much as is humanly possible, to triumph. And sometimes, as on the abandoned landing above the sea where Thurso died, the challenge is grappled:

> The platform is like a rough plank theatre-stage
> Built on the brow of the promontory: as if our blood had
>   labored all round the earth from Asia
> To play its mystery before strict judges at last, the final ocean
>   and sky, to prove our nature
> More shining than that of the other animals. It is rather
>   ignoble in its quiet times, mean in its pleasure,
> Slavish in the mass, but at stricken moments it can shine
>   terribly against the dark magnificence of things.[32]

In order to arrive at this restriction he had to retrace the development of religious consciousness to the point before Abraham—that is, before Revelation, and to dismiss Revelation as phantasy: racial delusion, the anthropomorphic trap. If the Christian cannot agree it is simply because he understands that all Jeffers intuits about divinity in the cosmos he intuits *as person*. When Revelation speaks, the correspondence is not anthropocentric only, for personality is itself trans-human, that is, is also angelic and divine. Because this is so Revelation, the intelligence from person to person, speaks with such incisiveness that to the Christian all the overwhelming efflux of the divine pulsing in the cosmos becomes diffuse and amorphous compared to the penetrating Voice he hears with such directness, and to which he responds. Be that as it may, Jeffers' primitive religious spirit and his elaborate scientific training between them absolved him from the task of grappling with the ontological constitution of personality. It follows from this that the chief liability of his doctrine was that it enabled him to brush aside contemptuously the strictest problems of existence; they became irrelevant, purely mental correlates of the basic human aberration; even as the chief asset was the incentive it gave him to celebrate the magnificent superfluity of the divine where humankind rarely chooses to recognize it.

But Jeffers knew the Voice. The residual Christian elements in his verse are unmistakable. Indeed, he was later to defend himself in terms of its directive:

> This is far from humanism; but it is in fact the Christian attitude:—to love God with all one's heart and soul, and one's neighbour as one's self: as much as that, but as *little* as that.[33]

If he seemed to close his ears perhaps it was in order to hear more clearly, from a quarter into which his father, for whom the Voice was all, could not intrude. If this is so it follows that his quarrel was not so much with the God of Revelation as with what men have made of Him.

Still, what is important to us is the poetry, and no matter how forbidding the philosophy, or how disturbing the religion, Jeffers will be read. Because man, in Emerson's phrase, "never so often deceived, still watches for the arrival of a brother who can *hold him steady to a truth until he has made it his own*."[34] If this is the poet's function, and I believe it is, then Robinson Jeffers has few equals in our time.

(1) Tocqueville, Alexis de, "What Causes Democratic Nations to Incline Towards Pantheism?" *Democracy in America* (New York, 1954), vol. II, pg. 32.

[In democracies] the idea of unity so possesses man and is sought by him so generally that if he thinks he has found it, he readily yields himself to that belief. Not content with the discovery that there is nothing in the world but a creation and a Creator, he is still embarrassed by this primary division of things and seeks to expand and simplify his conception by including God and the universe in one great whole.

(2) "I am struck in California," wrote George Santayana to Porter Garnett in a letter dated August 15, 1911, "by the deep and almost religious affection which people have for nature and by the sensitiveness they show for its influences ... It is their spontaneous substitute for articulate art and articulate religion." (Bancroft Library, University of California at Berkeley.)

(3) Carpenter, Frederic I. *Robinson Jeffers* (New York, 1962), pg. 53.

Written by a specialist in American literature rather than by a specialist in the content of modern poetry, this book gains from its broad approach. Coming at the moment of Jeffers' death it profits by an overall view which no previous work on the poet afforded. Its judgments are balanced rather than intensive, they present rather than argue. It is the best introduction to the whole work of the poet that has so far appeared.

(4) Shapiro, Karl. *In Defence of Ignorance* (New York, 1960), pg. 227.

In response to the question, "What is the pattern of the poet's life style?" the author replied: "Of course, it would be nice to say like a California poet: I live in a house on a deserted cliff. I built the house of boulders which I tore from the bed of the Pacific with my bare hands. I don't see what difference it makes." These words were uttered, presumably, in the mid-fifties. Today any spokesman for the new generation would hold that unless a poetic idiom originates in an authentic life style it cannot escape preciosity.

(5) Jeffers, Robinson. *Selected Letters* (Baltimore, 1968), pg. 7.

(6) Ibid., pg. 209.

(7) "Margrave," *The Selected Poetry of Robinson Jeffers* (New York, 1938), pg. 365.

(8) Emerson, Ralph Waldo. "The Method of Nature," *The Complete Writings of Ralph Waldo Emerson* (New York, 1929), pg. 65.

(9) "Margrave," *Selected Poetry*, pg. 370.

(10) *Complete Writings*, pg. 64.

(11) *Selected Poetry*, pg. 371.

(12) "Not Our Good Luck," *Roan Stallion, Tamar & Other Poems* (New York, 1925), pg. 242. Why Jeffers excluded this powerful poem from the *Selected Poetry* is difficult to say.

(13) By Perry Miller in his *The American Transcendentalists* (New York, 1957), pg. xi.

(14) Bennett, Melba Berry. *The Stone Mason of Tor House* (Los Angeles, 1966), pg. 118.

(15) *The Women at Point Sur*, pg. 9.

"But why should I make fables again? There are many
Tellers of tales to delight women and the people. I have no vocation."

(16) Powell, Lawrence Clark. *Robinson Jeffers: The Man And His Work* (Pasadena, 1940), pg. 45. (Second Edition.)

Written in the early thirties when Jeffers' reputation was at its zenith this, the first book-length study, is free from the painful necessity of defence and justification which so strains all subsequent efforts. Powell remains the poet's most palpable reader; his first qualification is that he manifestly likes what he reads, a rare gift in a critic, and his spontaneous accessibility to the poems makes his quotations exciting as well as illustrative. It is to be hoped that the famous librarian and bookman will close his career as he opened it, with what could be the final (as this is the initial) summary of the achievement of Robinson Jeffers.

(17) Winters, Yvor. "Robinson Jeffers," in *Literary Opinion in America*, by Morton Dawen Zabel (New York, 1937), pg. 247.

I have quoted from Zabel's anthology rather than from Winters' *In Defence of Reason* in order to present the essay as it originally appeared in *Hound & Horn*. Winters later retracted his approval of the lines terminating the eagle's apotheosis, and retained it only for those about the seals at dawn:

> Before the cock crew dawn
> Sea-lions began barking and coughing far off
> In the hollow ocean; but one screamed out like torture
> And bubbled under the water . . .

It is doubtful if any but the most dedicated practitioners of the late Stanford professor's method can say why these lines are better than a hundred others in the poem.

(18) Waggoner, Hyatt H. *American Poets, From the Puritans to the Present* (New York, 1968), pg. 476.

This book is *the* breakthrough study of American poetry done since the inception of the Modernist period. Jeffers, though, Waggoner decidedly misreads. Speaking of Lucretius' gods he says:

> Like them, Jeffers' God is capricious, unconcerned, and irrelevant. Unlike them, though, He does have one function wherever He appears; He is useful for attaching ultimate blame to. What kind of a God, Jeffers keeps asking, would it be that would make *this* kind of world?

Rather, Jeffers is asking precisely the opposite: What kind of world have *we* made which in its blindness refuses to see and acknowledge so stupendous a God? Although unfriendly to Jeffers, Waggoner's overview of our poetic heritage is a tremendous corrective to the dominant school of criticism since the advent of the Age of Eliot.

(19) Squires, Radcliffe. *The Loyalties of Robinson Jeffers* (Ann Arbor, 1957), pgs. 166–7.

Radcliffe Squires is the youngest of the writers who have attempted book-length studies of Jeffers' work. Writing in the mid-fifties when the poet's reputation was at its nadir he strove with great perspicacity against the dominant literary prejudice to affect a rehearing of Jeffers' claims. This effort often betrays him into a kind of self-conscious critical archness. But his insights are keen, he is a practicing poet with full awareness of modern aesthetic consciousness, and his struggle to take the measure of Jeffers' intellectual sources has not been equaled.

(20) These darker regions are the creative intoxication of the true dionysiac, which he enters in such masterpieces as *Tamar* and *The Women at Point Sur*. As Emerson says: "I think nothing is of any value in books excepting the transcendental and extraordinary. If a man is inflamed and carried away by his thought, to that degree that he forgets the authors and public and heeds only this one dream which holds him like an insanity, let me read his [poem], and you may have all the arguments and histories and criticism." ("The Poet," in *Complete Writings*, pg. 248.)

(21) Gilbert, Rudolf. *Shine, Perishing Republic* (Boston, 1936), pg. 93.

The least satisfying of the book-length studies of Jeffers' work, *Shine, Perishing Republic* is chiefly interesting for a phenomenal multiplicity of references. Were it better written it could accommodate this superfluity, but too many sentences like "The poet here has cast a final seal of approbation upon the imaginative powers of his genius" nullify his points.

(22) "The Tragic," in *Complete Writings*, pg. 1370.

(23) Ibid., pg. 1371.

(24) Idem.

(25) Idem.

(26) Emerson, pg. 1371.

(27) Ibid., pg. 1371.

(28) Quoted by Gilbert, op. cit., pg. 122.

(29) Monjian, Mercedes Cunningham. *Robinson Jeffers: A Study in Inhumanism* (Pittsburgh, 1958), pg. 88.

Falling chronologically between the studies of Squires and Carpenter, this shorter treatise is a judicious summary. She tends to see the poetry, magnificent as it is, as not sustaining the philosophy, rather than seeing the philosophy, as Powell does, as essentially a catalyst in the production of such poetry. But I for one shall always be grateful for the paragraph quoted. No one else said it before, and it is an observation of the first importance.

(30) Carpenter, op cit., pg. 86.

Once again I find myself somewhat apart from the "general consent" of the commentators. Whatever else in *Solstice* fails, and much does, it never fails its mood. This cannot be said for some of the other minor narratives.

(31) Kitto, H. D. F. *Greek Tragedy* (Garden City, 1954), pg. 208.

(32) "Thurso's Landing," *Selected Poetry*, pg. 357.

(33) Bennett, op. cit., pg. 185.

(34) "The Poet," in *Complete Writings*, pg. 241.

Cawdor

I

In nineteen-nine a fire swept our coast hills,
But not the canyons oceanward; Cawdor's ranges
And farm were safe. He had posted sentinels,
His son George and his man Jesus Acanna,
On two hills, and they watched the fire all night
Stream toward Cachagua; the big-coned inland pines
Made pillars of white flame.

                              Cawdor at dawn
Stood by his door and saw in the bronze light
That leaked through towers of smoke windowed with sanguine
Reflections of the burning, two does and a fawn
Spring down the creek-bed stones of his ravine
Fleeing from their terror, and then a tawny mountain-lion
With no eyes for the deer. Next walked a lame
Gray horse, a girl led it, a broken old man,
His face bound with a dirty cloth, clung weakly
To the limping withers. Cawdor recognized him
Though he was faceless, old Martial, who had got a place
In the hills two years before, a feeble old man
Marked for misfortune; his stock, the first year, sickened
With lump-jaw; when a cow died in the creek
Martial had let her lie there. Then Cawdor had ridden
And cursed him, and Cawdor with his man Acanna
Roped the horns to draw the carcass out of the stream,
But when they drew, it burst.
Now Martial came, he and his daughter Fera,

For refuge, having saved from the fire nothing
But their own lives and the lame horse.

                                    The old man
Reeled and was dumb with pain, but the girl asked
For Hood Cawdor, and Cawdor said "Not here.
He left last winter." Hood was his second son,
The hunter, with whom he had quarrelled. And Fera Martial:
"We've come," she pointed toward the smoke-towers, "from that.
You are Hood's father. You've the same drooping eyes, like
     a big animal's
That never needs to look sideways. I'm sorry, you'll have to take
     us in. My father is burnt, he is blinded.
The fire was on us before we awoke. He tried to fetch a bridle
     out of the burning stable.
There was a drum of coal-oil against the wall exploded and blew
     fire over his face.
I dragged him out of the fire." He said "Bring him in." "It wasn't
     dark," she answered, "the oaks were like torches,
And all the hill roared like a wave. He says we can go in, father,
     here is the door-step."
The old man groaned, lifting his hand to his face but not touching
     it, and hung back from the door.
"I wish to God you had left me at home." She said, "Your
     home?" "To be a blackened log with the others
Lying quiet," he said, "in the burnt hollow under the hill,
     and not have any care and not come
Blind and crying to my enemy's place." He turned in her hands
     and said "Oh Fera, where is the sun?
Is it afternoon?" She stood and held him. "Dear, only dawn.
     I think it must have come up, it's hidden
In the hell of smoke." "Turn me that way before I go in,
To the good light that gave me so many days. I have failed,
     and failed, and failed. Now I'll go in
As men go into the grave, and not fail any more."

4

He was in fact passive from that time on,
Except the restlessness of pain in bed
While his face scarred and the eyes died in the dark.
After the pain was lulled he seemed content
With blindness, it made an end of labor.

                                    Cawdor meanwhile
Would somehow have sent him up coast to Monterey
To find other charity; but the girl Fera
Coming ragged and courageous out of the fire
With cool gray eyes, had troubled his tough heart.
He'd not seen her before that dawn; and the image
Of the young haggard girl streaked with the dirt of the fire
And her skirt torn to bandage her father's face
Lived like a plant in his blood. He was fifty years old,
And mocked at himself; she was nineteen, she said.
But being a beggar really, under the burden
Of that blind man to care for, discounted youth;
And Cawdor, whatever the next ten years might bring him,
Felt no weight in the fifty. He had been stronger
From his youth up than other men, and still
The strength seemed to increase, the only changes
Toward age were harder lines in the shaven face
And fewer ferocities; the black passions of anger
That used to blind him sometimes had almost ceased.
Perhaps for lack of cause, now the few people
He dealt with knew him too well to cross him. And he'd security
And rough abundance to offer.

                            When Martial was able
Fera led him out-doors about the house
To feel the sun. He said it had no solidness
So near the ocean. "At home in the dear cup of the hills it used
    to come down

Like golden hammers, yet I'm content. Now it's dulled. Is there
    a cloud?" She answered, "Cypresses planted
Around the house, but the wind has broken them so . . .. Sit on this
    bench by the door, here it beats golden."
He sat, and soon handled a thing beside him on the warm
    plank. "What's this thing on the bench,
Like a saucer with little holes?" "An old sea-shell," she answered,
    "an abalone's. They grow on the ocean-reef;
All this black soil's full of their shells, the Indians brought
    up." He said: "Fera: while we stay here
Will you do something to lengthen the life you saved?
    When's the new moon? Go down when the tides drain out
In the dark of the moon and at full moon, gather me mussels
    and abalones, I'll drink the broth
And eat the meat, it is full of salts and nourishment. The ancestors
    of our life came from the sea
And our blood craves it, it will bring me years of health."
    She answered, "He wants us to go to-morrow." "Go, where?"
"That I can't tell. Is the sun pleasant?" "Oh, we can't go," he said,
    "you needn't be troubled. The sun
Is faint but pleasant. Now is that Cawdor passing?" "No. Concha
    Rosas," she answered. "She helps the cook.
She helped me when you were sick."

                                    Fera with private thoughts
Watched the Indian-blooded woman about her work
Pass in the dooryard, and go after a moment,
Carrying a pan under her arm, to the halved cask
Against the lift of the hill, where water trickled
From a wood pipe; tall weeds and calla lilies
Grew in the mud by it; the dark fat woman
Sat on a stone among them, paring and washing
Whatever was in the pan; and Fera said carefully:
"She has a child with blue eyes and she is an Indian.
She and the boy had their rooms in the house

When we came here, but Mr. Cawdor has moved them
To the old adobe out-building where Acanna
Lives with his wife." Her father listened or not, and answered: "Fera,
Am I still in the sun?" "Oh? Yes." "It is faint," he said,
    "but pleasant. I suppose now you can see the ocean
With golden scales on the broad blue?" "No," she answered,
    "we face up the canyon, toward the dark redwoods."

Cawdor's daughter Michal came by,
A blue-eyed girl of fourteen, nearly as tall as Fera.
She had a trap in her hand, and a live ground-squirrel
Dangled from it by the crushed paws. Then Fera
Left her father a moment to go with Michal
To the eagle's cage, to watch the captive be fed.
Against a cypress, a wide wire-screened box; no perch in it
But a wood block, for the bird's wing was broken.
Hood Cawdor, Michal's brother, had shot it, the autumn
Before he went away, and Michal had kept it alive.

She laid the squirrel inside and opened the trap.
The girls, their arms lacing each other's shoulders,
Set their faces against the wire to watch
The great dark-feathered and square-shouldered prisoner
Move in his corner One wide wing trailed through filth
Quickening a buzz of blow-flies; the fierce dark eyes
Had dropped their films, "He'll never be tame," Michal said
    sadly.
They watched the squirrel begin to drag its body
On the broken fore-paws. The indomitable eyes
Seemed never to have left the girls' faces but a grim hand
Came forward and gathered its prey under its talons.
They heard a whispering twitter continue
Below the hover of the dark plumes, until
The brown hackles of the neck bowed, the bleak head
Stooped over and stilled it.

Fera turned at a shadow
And saw Cawdor behind her, who said "One thing it's good for,
It makes Michal catch squirrels. Well, Fera, you're ready
    to go to-morrow?" "Let me go back to my father,"
She said, "I've left him alone too long. No, we're not ready."
    He followed her; Michal remained.
She touched her father's hand and spoke of the sun.
Old Martial lifted his cloth face, that he wore
To hide the scars; his voice dulled through the cloth:
"It is faint but very pleasant. I've been asleep."
She said "Mr. Cawdor's here." And Cawdor: "How are you.
    Now that he's better, Fera, little Romano
(That's Concha Rosas' boy) could take him walking
    in the afternoons and let you have a free time
To ride with Michal. If you could stay here. It's pitiful to see youth
    chained to helpless old age.
However, I have to drive to Monterey in the morning.
    I've put it off as long as I could,
And now he's able." She looked at Cawdor's face and his hands,
    and said "He means, father, that we
Must go to-morrow. I told you." Who sighed and answered,
    "That would be a long journey for nothing at all.
Are people more kind there? Wherever an old pitiful blind
    man goes
Someone will have to lead him and feed him and find
    him a bed. The world is not so made, Fera,
That he could starve. There *is* a God, but in human kindness."
    Cawdor said gravely: "Now's the other fool's turn
To speak: it makes me mad to have to spread out my foolishness.
I never had time to play with colored ribbons, I was brought
    up hard. I did a man's work at twelve
And bossed a gang at eighteen. That gets you nowhere. I learned
    that ruling poor men's hands is nothing,
Ruling men's money's a wedge in the world. But after I'd split
    it open a crack I looked in and saw

The trick inside it, the filthy nothing, the fooled and rotten faces
    of rich and successful men.
And the sons they have. Then I came down from the city.
I saw this place and I got it. I was what you call honest
    but I was hard; the little Mexican
Cried when I got it. A canyon full of redwoods and hills
    guaranteed not to contain gold.
I'd what I wanted, and have lived unshaken. My wife died when
    Michal was born; and I was sorry,
She seemed frightened at the end; but life was not changed.
I am fifty years old, the boys have grown up; and now I'm caught
    with wanting something and my life is changed.
I haven't slept for some nights. You'd think I might have been
    safe at fifty. Oh, I'm still my own master
And will not beg anything of you. Old blind man your girl's
    beautiful, I saw her come down the canyon
Like a fawn out of the fire. If she is willing: if you are willing,
    Fera, this place is yours.
It's no palace and no kingdom: but you are a beggar. It might
    be better for you to live
In a lonely place than lead your old blind-man up the cold street
And catch dimes in his hat. If you're not willing:
I'll tell you something. You are not safe here, by God you're
    not. I've been my own master;
But now I'm troubled with two wolves tearing each other:
    to kneel down like a fool and worship you,
And the other thing." She whitened and smiled. "I'm not afraid:
    but I'm not experienced. Marriage you mean?
There's no security in anything less. We are, as you say, beggars:
    we want security." Old Martial
Groped and muttered against her. She laughed: "I'm driving
    a bargain: be quiet, father." Cawdor said sadly:
"I think that I am the one being made a fool of, old man, not you.
    Fera, if you were willing

We'd drive up and be married to-morrow. And then . . . there
     must be something . . . clothes, clothes: you look ridiculous
Bursting through Michal's like the bud of a poppy." She stood
     quietly and looked over the dooryard
At Concha Rosas peeling potatoes beside the fountain. "Who's
     that wide-lapped dark o' the moon
Among the lilies?" He said, "Why: Concha. You know her."
     "Oh, Concha. And now you've moved her out of the house."
"Yes," he said angrily. And Fera laughing: "There is nothing
     under the sun worth loving but strength: and I
Had some but it's tired, and now I'm sick of it. I want
     you to be proud and hard with me; I'm not tame
If you ever soften. Oh, yes, to your offer. I'd a friend once that
     had fine dreams, she didn't look forward
Into her mist of moon on the roses—not Rosas—you remember
     Edith,
Father?—with half the heart that races me to meet to-morrow."
     Than Cawdor shuddered with hope of love;
His face relaxing began to look like an old man's. He stooped
     toward Fera, to fondle or kiss,
She drew herself back. "Not now. Oh, I'll be honest
And love you well." She took her father by the arm. "The sun's
     passed from the bench, father, come in.
I'll build a fire on the hearth if you want." And Cawdor: "That's
     it! You like horses, that's what I'll give you.
You liked mine but I'll buy you better; Morales has a pair
     of whites as beautiful as flowers.
We'll drive by there to-morrow. Like kittens they are." He followed
     her in-doors.

Blue kingfisher laughing, laughing in the lit boughs
Over lonely water,
Is there no man not duped and therefore you are laughing?
No strength of a man

10

But falls on folly before it drops into dust?
Go wicked arrow down to the ocean
And learn of gulls: they laugh in the cloud, they lament also.
The man who'd not be seduced, not in hot youth,
By the angel of fools, million-worshipped success,
The self-included man, the self-armored,
And never beguiled as to a bull nor a horse,
Now in his cooled and craglike years
Has humbled himself to beg pleasure: even power was better.
Laugh kingfisher, laugh, that is their fashion.
Whoever has discerned the vanity of water will desire wind.

II

The night of Cawdor's marriage, his son
Hood Cawdor lay in the north on the open sand-beach
Of a long lake. He was alone; his friend in that country
Who hunted with him, had gone to the Indian camp.
Hood slept beside his fire and seemed to awake
And hear the faint ripple, and wind in far firs,
Then all at once a voice came from the south
As if it had flown mountains and wide valleys yet clearly heard
And like a dying man's, "Hood, Hood. My son." He saw
His father's face clearly a moment after
Distorted either with pain or approached of death.
But then the actual stars of the night came through it,
Like those of a winter evening, Orion rising,
Altair and Vega going west. When he remembered
It was early autumn, he knew it must be past midnight.
He laid a flare of twigs on the live coals
Before he lay down; eyes on the opposite shore
Would have seen the sharp stars in the black crystal
Of the lake cancelled by a red comet's tail.

That night and in the morning Hood had no doubt
His father had just died, or approached death;
But dreams and visions are an obscure coinage
No sane person takes faithfully. He thought of writing
To his sister Michal; he had no habit of writing.
Months later, after the rains began and cramped
His migrant hunting, he thought not with much sorrow
Yet mournfully, of his father as dead; and thought
That he'd a share in the place unless he'd been,
As appeared likely, cut off by a written will.
No doubt it was too late to see the old man,
Yet he'd go south. He sold his horse and shot-gun, took his rifle
    and went south.

                    He approached home
Over the hills, not by the coast-road from Monterey. Miles
    beyond miles a fire had devoured,
Until he looked from the height into the redwood canyons
    pitching to the ocean, these were unhurt,
Dark green and strong. Then he believed his father could
    not have died.

                The first canyon he entered,
A mountain-lion stood stilted on a bare slope between alder
    and redwood watching him come down:
Like the owner of the place: he slid the rifle-stock to his cheek,
    thinking "The hills have not been hunted
Since I've been gone"; he fired, and the lank August-pasture-
    colored body somersaulted
Over the ridge; he found it lying under a laurel-bush. The skinning
    was a long toil; Hood came
Burdened across the fall of twilight to the great dome
    of high-cliffed granite, they call it the Rock,
That stands out of the hill at the head of Cawdor's canyon.

Here, after
the trivial violent quarrel
That sped him from home the year before, he had built a fire
at dusk hoping Michal would see it
And come to bid him good-bye; she had seen and come. He stood
now and saw, down the great darkening gorge,
The reddish-yellow windows glimmer in his father's house,
the iron-dark ocean a bank beyond,
Pricked at the gray edge with one pin-point ship's light. Deep,
vast, and quiet and sad. After a little
He gathered sticks under the oaks and made a fire on the Rock's
head, wishing Michal might see it.
If not, he could go down in the morning, (he'd blanket and food)
and see whether the place was changed.

Michal had gone in-doors but Acanna saw it,
A bright high blood-drop under the lump-shaped moon,
When he was stamping stable-yard muck from his boots
Before he went in to supper. He said to the new farmhand
Dante Vitello, the Swiss whom Cawdor had brought
From Monterey: "You seen strangers go through?
Some fellow's got a fire on the Rock." Then Michal
Hurried her meal and went out. The fire waned,
Rayless red star up the blue-shadow-brimming
Moon-silver-lipped gorge. Michal went doubtfully
Up the dim moon-path by the lone redwood that lately
Excited by her father's marriage
She'd made a secret marriage with, and a law
That she must always touch it in passing. She touched it
Without much ceremony, and climbed, and peered
Under the oaks at the man out on the Rock's head.
Oh, it was Hood, in the red ember-glow. They met gladly;
The edge of shadow and moon-gleam down the gulf of the canyon
crept up out of sight
Under the Rock before she went home. Hood said "You'll
ask the old man whether he'd like to see me.

13

But tell him that I'll not stay. No plowing, I'm not a farmer."
"You're still only a hunter," she answered.

By the house under the broken cypresses;
The saffron dawn from which Hood had descended
Still hung in the V of the canyon; Cawdor with morning
    friendliness, "Stay for a week if you like. Don't fear,
I won't set you at plowing, we've done the plowing. My wife's
    father," he said, "has your old room,
But you can have the one on the north, used to be Concha's."
    Fera Martial came out; she had changed
Amazingly from the sallow girl that Hood
Had seen two years ago at the lean farm. The eyes had not changed.
    A wind blew from her eyes
Like sea-wind from the gray sea. "Here's Hood," said Cawdor.
    "He looks more like you," she said, "than either of the others."
"As long as you don't ask him to work. George works, but this
Is only a hunter. Let him have the little north room for a week."
    Hood unstrapped the raw stiffening
Puma-skin from his pack. "I owe you a wedding-present,"
    he said to Fera, "if you'll take this
I'll get it tanned. I shot it yesterday." Fera took in both hands
    the eight-foot trophy, she made
To draw it over her shoulders, "Stop. It's not dry, you'll stain
    your dress." "Who am I," she said impatiently,
"Not to be stained?" She assumed it like a garment, the head
    with the slits for eyes hung on her breast,
The moonstone claws dangling, the glazed red fleshy under-side
Turned at the borders, her bare forearm crossing it. "Sticky,"
    she said and took it in-doors. "Come in."
He carried his pack, she led him up-stairs to the north room.
    "This was not yours when you used to live here."
"No. Mine was where your father is now." "Then who had this
    one?"

He answered "I don't remember: nobody: I guess it was empty."
"That Rosas woman," she answered, "had it.
But the bed's aired." She left him there and went down.

He went out-doors to find Michal again
And couldn't find her; he wandered about and played with
    the horses,
Then Michal was coming up from the field seaward.
She carried a trap in her hand, and a live ground-squirrel
Dangled from it by the crushed paws, the white-rimmed
Eyes dull with pain, it had lain caught all night.
"What's that, Michal, why don't you kill it?" "A treat
    for the eagle.
I've taught him to eat beef but he loves to kill.
Oh, squirrels are scarce in winter." "What, you've still
    got the eagle?"
"Yes. Come and watch."

                    Hood remembered great sails
Coasting the hill and the redwoods. He'd shot for the breast,
But the bird's fate having captivity in it
Took in the wing-bone, against the shoulder, the messenger
Of human love; the broad oar of the wing broke upward
And stood like a halved fern-leaf on the white of the sky,
Then all fell wrecked. He had flung his coat over its head,
Still the white talon-scars pitted his forearm.

The cage was not in the old place. "Fera," she said,
"She made me move it because it smells. I can't
Scrape the wood clean." Michal had had it moved
To the only other level on the pitch of the hill;
The earth-bench a hundred feet above the house-roof,
An old oak's roots partly upheld; a faint
Steep path trailed up there. One side of the low leaning

Bole of the tree was the eagle's cage, on the other
A lichened picket-fence guarded two graves,
Two wooden head-boards. Cawdor's dead wife was laid here
Beside a child that had died; an older sister
Of Hood's and Michal's.

                              They stood and watched
The dark square-shouldered prisoner, the great
     flight-feathers
Of the dragged wing were worn to quills, and beetles
Crawled by the weaponed feet, yet the dark eyes
Remembered their pride. Hood said "You ought
     to kill him.
My God, nearly two years!" She answered nothing,
But when he looked at her face the long blue eyes
Winked and were brimmed. The grim hand took
     the squirrel,
It made a whispering twitter, the bleak head tore it,
And Michal said "George wanted to kill him too.
I can't let him be killed. And now, day after day,
I have to be cruel to bring him a little happiness."
Hood laughed; they stood looking down on the house,
All roof and dormers from here, among the thirteen
Winter-battered cypresses planted about it.

          III

The next day's noon Michal said, "Her old father
Believes that food from the sea keeps him alive.
The low tides at full moon we always go down."
When Fera came they took sacks for the catch

16

And brown iron blades to pry the shells from the rock.
They went to the waste of the ebb under the cliff,
Stone wilderness furred with dishevelled weed, but under
    each round black-shouldered stone universes
Of color and life, scarlet and green sea-lichens, violet
    and rose anemones, wave-purple urchins,
Red starfish, tentacle-rayed pomegranate-color sun-disks, shelled
    worms tuft-headed with astonishing
Flower-spray, pools of live crystal, quick eels plunged in the crevices
    ... the three intrusive atoms of humanity
Went prying and thrusting; the sacks fattened with shell-vaulted
    meat. Then Fera said "Go out on the reef,
Michal, and when you've filled the sack with mussels call Hood
    to fetch it." "Why should I go? Let *him*."
"Go Michal, I need Hood to turn over the stones." When Michal
    was gone
And walked beyond hearing on the low reef, dim little remote
    figure between the blind flat ocean
And burning sky, Fera stood up and said suddenly: "Judge
    me, will you. Kindness is like ...
The slime on my hands, I want judgment. We came out of the
    mountain fire beggared and blinded,
Nothing but a few singed rags and a lame horse
That has died since. Now you despise me because I gave myself
    to your father. Do then: I too
Hate myself now, we've learned he likes dark meat—that
    Rosas—a rose-wreath of black flesh for his bride
Was not in the bargain. It leaves a taste." Hood steadied himself
    against the wind of her eyes, and quietly:
"Be quiet, you are telling me things that don't concern me, true
    or not. I am not one of the people that live
In this canyon." "You can be cold, I knew that, that's Cawdor.
    The others have kindly mother in them.
Wax from the dead woman: but when I saw your face I knew
    it was the pure rock. I loved him for that.

For I did love him, he is cold and strong. So when you judge
   me, write in the book that she sold herself
For someone to take care of her blind father, but not without
   love. You had better go out on the reef
And help Michal."

                     He went, and kneeling beside his sister
   to scrape the stiff brown-bearded lives
From the sea face of the rock, over the swinging streaks of foam
   on the water, "Michal," he said,
"I wish you could get free of this place. We must think what
   we can do. God knows I wouldn't want you
Like the girls in town, pecking against a shop-window." "What
   did she want to tell you?" "Nothing at all.
Only to say she loves the old man. Michal, keep your mind
   clean, be like a boy, don't love.
Women's minds are not clean, their mouths declare it, the shape
   of their mouths. They want to belong to someone.
But what do I know? They are all alike to me as mussels."
   The sack was filled; reluctance to return
Had kept him hewing at the thick bed of mussels, letting them
   slide on the rock and drop in the water,
When he looked up Fera had come. "Why do you waste them?"
   she said. "You're right, waste is the purpose
And value of . . . Look, I've something to waste." She extended
   her hand toward him, palm downward, he saw bright blood
Trickle from the tips of the brown fingers and spot the rock.
   "You're hurt?" "Oh, nothing. I turned a stone,
A barnacle cut me, you were so long coming I thought I could
   do without you. Well, have you judged me,
With Michal to help?" "Let me see the cut," he said angrily.
   She turned the gashed palm cup-shape upward
On purpose to let a small red pool gather. She heard his teeth
   grating, that pleased her. He said

18

"I can't see," then she flung it on the ocean. "But you're a hunter,
   you must have seen many a wild creature
Drain, and not paled a shade." He saw the white everted lips
   of the cut and suffered a pain
Like a stab, in a peculiar place. They walked
And were silent on the low reef; Hood carried the sea-lymph-
   streaming sack on his shoulder. Every third step
A cold and startling shadow was flung across them; the sun was
   on the horizon and the tide turning
The surf mounted, each wave at its height covered the sun. A river
   of gulls flowed away northward,
Long wings like scythes against the face of the wave, the heavy
   red light, the cold pulses of shadow,
The croaking voice of a heron fell from high rose and amber.

                                                    There
         were three sacks to bring up the cliff.
Hood sent his sister to fetch a horse to the cliffhead to carry them
   home, but Michal without an answer
Went home by herself, along the thread of gray fog
That ran up the great darkening gorge like the clue of a labyrinth.
   Hood, climbing, saw on the cliffhead, unreal
To eyes upward and sidelong, his head cramped by the load,
   like a lit pillar Fera alone
Waiting for him, flushed with the west in her face,
The purple hills at her knees and the full moon at her thigh,
   under her wounded hand new-risen.
He slid the sack on the grass and went down. His knees wavered
   under the second on the jags of rock,
Under the third he stumbled and fell on the cliffhead. They were
   not too heavy but he was tired. Then Fera
Lay down beside him, he laughed and stood up. "Where's Michal?
   I sent her to fetch a horse." And Fera shivering:
"I waited for you but Michal went on. My father says that life
   began in the ocean and crept

                                                    19

Like us, dripping sea-slime up the high cliff. He used
    to be a schoolmaster but mother left him,
She was much younger than he. Then he began to break himself
    on bad liquor. Our little farm
Was the last refuge. But he was no farmer. We had utterly failed
And fallen on hollow misery before the fire came. That sort
    of thing builds a wall against recklessness.
Nothing's worth risk; now I'll be mean and cautious all the rest
    of my life, grow mean and wrinkled
Sucking the greasy penny of security. For it's known beforehand,
    whatever I attempt bravely would fail.
That's in the blood. But see," she looked from the ocean sundown
    to the violet hills and the great moon,
"Because I choose to be safe all this grows hateful. What shall
    I do?" He said scornfully: "Like others,
Take what you dare and let the rest go." "That is no limit. I dare,"
    she answered. He looked aside
At the dark presence of the ocean moving its foam secretly below
    the red west, and thought
"Well, what does she want?" "Nothing," she said as if she had
    heard him. "But I wish to God
I were the hunter." She went up to the house,
And there for days was silent as a sheathed knife,
Attending her sick father and ruling the housework
With bitter eyes. At night she endured Cawdor if he pleased
As this earth endures man.

                                  A morning when no one
Was in the house except her father in his room,
She stole to Hood's room on the north to fall
On the open bed and nuzzle the dented pillow
With a fire face; but then sweating with shame
Rose and fetched water for some menial service
About her father's body; he had caught cold
And was helplessly bedfast again.

20

                              Meanwhile Hood Cawdor
With hunting deer at waterheads before dawn,
Evening rides with Michal, lucky shots at coyotes,
And vain lying-wait and spying of creekside pad-prints
For the great mountain-lion that killed a calf,
Contentedly used six days of his quick seven
And would have gone the eighth morning. But the sixth night
The farm-dogs yelled furious news of disaster,
So that Hood snatched up half his clothes and ran out
Barefoot; George came behind him; they saw nothing.
The dogs were silent, two of them came at call
Under the late moonrise cancelled with cloud,
But would not quest nor lead. Then the young men
Returned to bed. In the white of dawn they found
The dog that had not come in the night, the square-jawed
Fighter and best of the dogs, against the door
So opened with one stroke of an armed paw
That the purple entrails had come out, and lay
On the stone step, speckled with redwood needles.

That postponed Hood's departure, he was a hunter
And took the challenge. He found the fighting-spot,
Scratched earth and the dog's blood, but never the slayer.

IV

     A sudden rainstorm
Beat in from the north ocean up a blue heaven and spoiled
     his hunting. The northwest wind veered east
The rain came harder, in heavy falls and electric pauses. Hood
     had come home, he sat with Michal
Playing checkers; Fera was up-stairs with her father.

The blind man had grown feebler; he had been in fact dying
　　since the fire; but now two days he had eaten
Nothing, and his lungs clogged. Most of the daytime
And half the night Fera'd spent by his bedside. He had lain
　　deeply absorbed in his own misery,
His blindness concentrating his mood, until the electric streams
　　and hushes of the rain vexed him,
Toward evening he fell into feverish talk of trivial
Remembered things, little dead pleasures. Fera gave patient
　　answers until he slept. She then
Left him and slept heavily beside her husband.

　　　The rain had ceased, Hood saw a star from his window
And thought if the rain ceased he might give over his hunting
　　and go to-morrow. But out of doors
Was little promise of the rain ceasing; the east wind had slipped
　　south, the earth lay expectant. The house
Wore an iron stub for some forgotten purpose
Fixed upward from the peak of the roof; to one passing out-doors
　　at midnight the invisible metal
Would have shown a sphered flame, before the thunder began.

　　　Fera before the first thunderclap
Dreaming imagined herself the mountain-lion that had killed
　　the dog; she hid in leaves and the hunter
Aimed at her body through a gap in the green. She waited
　　the fire, rigid, and through closed lids
Saw lightning flare in the window, she heard the crash of the rifle.
　　The enthralling dream so well interpreted
The flash and the noise that she was not awakened but slept
　　to the second thunder. She rose then, and went
To her father's room for he'd be awakened. He was not awakened.
He snored in a new manner, puffing his cheeks. Impossible
　　to wake him. She called Cawdor. In the morning

22

They sent Acanna, for form's sake, not hope's, to fetch a doctor.
    Hood offered to ride, Acanna was sent.
The torrents of rain prevented his return, and the doctor's coming,
    to the third day. But northward
He rode lightly, the storm behind him.

                                The wind had shifted before
        dawn and grooved itself
A violent channel from east of south, the slant of the coast;
    the house-roof groaned, the planted cypresses
Flung broken boughs over the gables and all the lee slope
    of the gorge was carpeted green
With the new growth and little twigs of the redwoods.
    They bowed themselves at last, the redwoods, not shaken
By common storms, bowed themselves over; their voice and not
    the ocean's was the great throat of the gorge
That roared it full, taking all the storm's other
Noises like little fish in a net.

                        On the open pasture
The cattle began to drift, the wind broke fences.
But Cawdor, although unsure and thence in his times
Violent toward human nature, was never taken
Asleep by the acts of nature outside; he knew
His hills as if he had nerves under the grass,
What fence-lengths would blow down and toward what cover
The cattle would drift. He rode with George, and Hood
Rode after, thwart the current in the cracked oaks
To the open mercy of the hill. They felt the spray
And sharp wreckage of rain-clouds in the steel wind,
And saw the legs of the others' horses leaning
Like the legs of broken chairs on the domed rims
On the running sky.

                                            23

                    In the house Fera
Sat by her father's bed still as a stone
And heard him breathe, that was the master-noise of the house
That caught the storm's noises and cries in a net,
And captured her mind; the ruling tenth of her mind
Caught in the tidal rhythm lay inert and breathing
Like the old man's body, the deep layers left unruled
Dividing life in a dream. She heard not the roof
Crying in the wind, nor on the window
The endless rattle of earth and pebbles blasted
From the hill above. For hours; and a broken cypress bough
Rose and tapped the strained glass, at a touch the pane
Exploded inward, glass flew like sparks, the fury of the wind
Entered like a wild beast. Nothing in the room
Remained unmoved except the old man on the bed.

Michal Cawdor had crawled up the hill four-foot
To weight her eagle's cage with heavier stones
Against the storm, and creeping back to the house
Heard the glass crash and saw the gapped window.
      She got up-stairs
And saw in the eddying and half blinded glimmer
Fera's face like an axe and the window blocked
With a high wardrobe that had hidden the wall
Between the two windows, a weight for men
To strain at, but Fera whose nerves found action before
Her mind found thought had wrestled it into service
Instead of screaming, the instant the crash snapped her deep
      trance. When Michal came Fera was drawing
The table against the wardrobe to hold it firm, her back
      and shoulders flowing into lines like fire
Between the axe face and the stretched arms: "Ah, shut the door,"
      she said panting, "did Hood go with them?
He hasn't *gone*?" "Who? Hood?" "Coo if you like: has he gone?"
      "He went with father," she answered trembling,

24

"To herd the cows . . .." "Why are your eyes like eggs then,
    for he'll come back, Michal?" She went to the bedside
And murmured "He hasn't moved, it hasn't hurt him." But
    Michal: "Did you want Hood?" "Want him? I wanted
Someone to stop the window. Who could bear life
If it refused the one thing you want? I've made a shutter to hold
    although it sings at the edges.
Yet he felt nothing. Michal, it doesn't storm for a sparrow's
    death. You and I, Michal, won't have
A stir like this to speed us away in our times. He is dying."
    Michal answered, "Dante Vitello's
Roping the haystacks, I'll fetch him Fera?" "What could
    he do while the wind continues, more than I've done?
We can stand draughts. Oh Michal, a man's life and his soul
Have nothing in common. You never knew my father, he had eagle
    imaginations. This poor scarred face
For whose sake neither nature nor man has ever stepped from
    the path while he was living: his death
Breaks trees, they send a roaring chariot of storm to home him.
Hood wouldn't leave without his rifle," she said,
"He didn't take the rifle when he went up?"
"Why no, not in this wind."

                    In the afternoon the wind
Fell, and the spray in the wind waxed into rain.
The men came home, they boarded the broken window.
The rain increased all night. At dawn a high sea-bird,
If any had risen so high, watching the hoary light
Creep down to sea, under the cloud-streams, down
The many canyons the great sea-wall of coast
Is notched with like a murderer's gun-stock, would have seen
Each canyon's creek-mouth smoke its mud-brown torrent
Into the shoring gray; and as the light gained
Have seen the whole wall gleam with a glaze of water.

V

There was a little acre in Cawdor's canyon
Against the creek, used for a garden, because they could water it
In summer through a wood flume; but now the scour
Devoured it; and after Cawdor had ditched the barns
Against the shoreless flood running from the hill,
In the afternoon he turned to save this acre.
He drove piling to stay the embankment; Hood pointed
The beams, and Cawdor drove them with the great
    sledgehammer,
Standing to his knees in the stream.

                         Then Fera Cawdor
Came down the bank without a cloak, her hair
Streaming the rain, and stood among the brown leafless
And lavender shoots of willow. "Oh come to the house, Hood."
She struck her hands together. "My father is conscious,
He wants to speak to Hood, wants Hood." Who wondering
Gave the axe to his brother and went up.

                         They came
    to the room off the short hallway; he heard
Through the shut door before they reached it the old man's
    breathing: like nothing he'd ever heard in his life:
Slime in a pit bubbling: but the machine rhythm, intense
    and faultless. She entered ahead
And drew a cloth over the wrinkled eye-pits; the bald scars
    in the beard, and the open mouth,
Were not covered. "Ah shut the door," she said, "against the wind
    on the stairway." He came reluctantly
Into the dreadful rhythm of the room, and said "When
    was he conscious? He is not now." And Fera:

26

"He is in a dream: but *I* am in a dream, between blackness
and fire, my mind is never gathered,
And all the years of thoughtful wonder and little choices are gone.
He is on the shore of what
Nobody knows: but *I* am on that shore. It is lonely. I was the one
that needed you. Does he feel anything?"
He thought, this breathing-machine? "Why no, Fera."
"It is only because I am cold," she said wringing her hands,
violently trembling, "the cold rainwater
Rains down from my hair.
I hated my loose mother but this old man was always gentle
and good even in drunkenness.
Lately I had true delight in doing things for him, the feeding,
cleaning, we'd travelled so far together,
So many faces of pain. But now he has flown away, where
is it?" She mastered her shuddering and said
"All that I loved is here dying: and now if you should
ask me to I would strike his face
While he lies dying." But he bewildered in the ice-colored wind
of her eyes stood foolish without an answer,
And heard her: "Do you understand?" He felt the wind tempered,
it fell in tears, he saw them running
By the racked mouth; she ceased then to be monstrous and
became pitiful. Her power that had held him captive
Ceased also, and now he was meanly afraid of what she might
do. He went through the house and found Michal,
And brought her up to the room. Then Fera lifted her face from
the bed, and stood, and answered "Come Michal.
This is the place. Come and look down and despise us. Oh, we
don't mind. You're kind: I am wicked perhaps
To think that he is repulsive as well as pitiful to you. You hunter
with a rifle, one shot's
Mercy in the life: but the common hunter of the world uses
too many; wounds and not kills, and drives you
Limping and bleeding, years after years,

Down to this pit. One hope after another cracked in his hands;
    the school he had; then the newspaper
He labored day and night to build up, over in the valley. His wife,
    my shameful mother abandoned him.
He took whiskey for a friend, it turned a devil. He took the farm
    up here, hunted at last
To the mountain, and nothing grew, no rain fell, the cows died
Before the fire came. Then it took his eyes and now it is taking
    his life. Now it has taken
Me too, that had been faithful awhile. For I have to tell you, dear,
    dear Michal, before he dies,
I love you—and Hood for your sake, Michal—
More than I do this poor man. He lies abandoned." She stood
    above him, her thin wet clothing
In little folds glued to the flesh, like one of the girls in a Greek
    frieze, the air of their motion
Molds lean in marble; Michal saw her through mist in the eyes
    and thought how lovely she was, and dimly
Heard her saying: "Do you not wish you were like this
    man, Hood? *I* wish I were like this man.
He has only one thing left to do. It is great and maybe dreadful
    to die, but nothing's easier.
He does it asleep. Perhaps we *are* like this man: we have only
    one thing left to do, Hood,
One burning thing under the sun. I love you so much, Michal,
    that you will surely forgive
Whatever it is. You'll know it is not done wickedly, but only from
    bitter need, from bitter need . . .."
She saw him frowning, and Michal's wonder, and cried quickly:
"You needn't pity him! For even in this deformity and shame
    of obscure death he is much more fortunate
Than any king of fat steers: under the bone, behind the burnt
    eyes
There have been lightnings you never dreamed of, despairs and
    exultations and hawk agonies of sight

That would have cindered your eyes before the fire came.
Now leave me with him. If I were able I would take
     him up, groaning to death, to the great Rock
Over your cramp cellar of a canyon, to flame his bitter soul
     away like a shot eagle
In the streaming sky. I talk foolishly. Michal you mustn't come
     back until he has died, death's dreadful.
You're still a child. Stay, Hood." But he would not.

                                        He heard
          in the evening
The new farmhand talking with Concha Rosas,
His Alp-Italian accent against her Spanish-
Indian like pebbles into thick water. "This country
You cannot trust, it never need any people.
My old country at home she is not so kind
But always she need people, she never kill all.
She is our mother, can't live without us. This one not care.
It make you fat and soon it cutting your neck."
Concha answered inaudibly, and the other: "You Indian.
Not either you. I have read, you come from Ah-sia.
You come from Ah-sia, us from Europe, no one from here.
Beautiful *matrigna* country, she care for Indian
No more nor white nor black, how have she help you?"
Their talk knotted itself on miscomprehension
Until *matrigna* shaped into *madrastra*.
"Beautiful stepmother country."

                    Hood ceased to hear them.
Why, so she was. He saw as if in a vision
The gray flame of her eyes like windows open
To a shining sky the north wind sweeps, and wind
And light strain from the windows. What wickedness in the fabric
Was driving her mad with binding her to old men?
He went to the door to look at the black sky.

                                        29

He'd leave the house to-night but pity and the rain held him.
He heard the eaves gutter in their puddles and rush
Of rivulets washing the dark.

                                    While he was there
She came from the stair and whispered: for they were alone
In the dark room, the others in the lamplit room
At the table: "If I were hurt in the hills,
Dying without help, you'd not sneak off and leave me.
Oh, nobody could do that. Pull the door to
On that black freedom. Perhaps my father will die
This drowning night, but can't you see that I am a prisoner
Until he does: the wrists tied, the ankles:
I can neither hold nor follow.
No, no, we have to let them take their time dying.
Why, even on Cawdor's, on your father's account
It would be wicked to call despair in here
Before it must come. I might do strangely
If I were driven. You'll promise. Put your hand here."
She caught it and held it under the small breast
Against the one dry thinness of cloth. She had changed then.
He felt it thudding. "I am being tortured you know."
He shook and said "Until he dies I'll not go.
Dear child, then you'll be quieter." "When you said *child*,
Your voice," she answered, "was as hard as your father's.
Hood, listen, all afternoon
I have been making a dream, you know my two white horses,
They are like twins, they mustn't be parted.
One for you, one for me, we rode together in the dream
Far off in the deep world, no one could find us.
We leaned and kissed . . ." He thrust her off, with violent fear,
And felt her throat sob in his hand, the hot slender
Reed of that voice of hers, the drumming arteries

Each side the reed flute. She went crouching and still
To the stair; he stood in the dark mourning his violence.

But she had gone up into the snoring rhythm
Neither day nor night changed. Cawdor had asked her
Whom she would have to watch with her all night,
"For you must sleep a little." She had chosen Concha
Rosas; and that was strange, he thought she had always
Hated Concha. He came at the end of evening
And brought the brown fat silent woman.

                              Then Fera
Looked up, not rising from the chair by the bed,
And said with a difficult smile over the waves of noise:
"I was thinking of a thing that worried my father, in the old days.
    He made a bargain with a man
To pasture his horse, the horse died the first week. The man came
    asking pay for a year's pasture
For a dead horse. My father paid it at last, I wouldn't have paid
    it." "No, hardly," he answered. And Fera:
"The bargain ends when the man dies—when the horse dies."
    She looked at her dying father and said
Shuddering: "I'm sorry to keep you up all night, Concha;
    but you can sleep in your chair. He was always
A generous fool, he wasn't made for this world." Cawdor looked
    down at the bed through the dull noise
Like surf on a pebble shore, and said that he'd been out to look
    at the bridge; it was still standing.
The rain would break to-night, the doctor would come to-morrow.
    "That would be late, if there were hope,"
She answered, "no matter." "Dear child," he said hoarsely,
    "we all die." "Those that have blood in us. When you said *child*,

Your voice," she answered, "was as hard as a flint. We know that
    you and the Rock over the canyon
Will not die in our time. When they were little children
Were you ever kind?" "Am I not now?" "Oh, kind." She leaned
    sidewise and smoothed
The coverlet on the bed, but rather as a little hawk slips sidelong
    from its flapping vantage
In the eye of the wind to a new field. "But about blood
    in the stone veins, could Concha tell me?
Look, his face now Concha, pure rock: a flick and it shows.
    Oh," she said and stood up, "forgive me.
For I am half mad with watching him
Die like an old steer the butcher forgot. It makes me
Mad at your strength. He had none: but his mind had shining
    wings, they were soon broken."

                                        When Cawdor went out
She said to Concha, "It is growing cold. Wrap yourself
    in the blanket before you sleep in the chair."
When Concha nodded she went and shook her awake,
    by the fat shoulder. "Did Hood make love to anyone
In those old days? They're hot at sixteen." "He never. Oh no."
    "You didn't serve the father and the sons?
Whom did he love?" "Nobody. He love the deer
He's only a boy and he go hunting." Fera whispered from
    the throat: "I wish to God, you brown slug,
That I had been you, to scrape the mud from his boots when
    he came in from hunting: or Ilaria Acanna
Cooking him little cakes in the oak-smoke, in the white dawns
    when the light shakes like water in a cup
And the hills are foam: for now who knows what will
    happen?
Oh sleep, cover your head with the blanket, nothing has
    changed."

32

She went about the room and rested in her chair.
The snoring rhythm took her mind captive again,
And in a snatch of sleep she dreamed that Michal
Had stolen her lion-skin, the one that Hood had given her,
And wore it in the hills and was shot for a lion.
Her dead body was found wrapped in the skin.
There was more, but this was remembered.

                                    Perhaps the minds
That slept in the house were wrought to dreams of death
By knowledge of the old man's ebbing. Hood Cawdor
Dreamed also of a dead body; he seemed a child; at first
He dreamed it was his father lay dead in the house,
But afterwards his father held him by the hand
Without a break in the dream. They looked through a door
Into the room in which his mother lay dead.
There an old woman servant, who had now been gone
These many years, prepared his mother's body
For burial; she was washing the naked corpse.
Matrigna; madrastra. He awoke and lay in the dark
Gathering his adult mind, assuring himself
The dream grew from no memory; he remembered
His mother living, nothing of seeing her dead.
Yes, of the burial a little; the oak on the hill,
And the red earth. His thought of the grave calmed him
So that he was falling asleep.

                              But Fera remained awake
After her dream. How could one drive a wedge
Between the father and the son? There was not now
Any affection: but Hood was loyal: or afraid.
They had quarrelled the time before. The snatch of sleep
Had cleared her mind.

She heard the snoring rhythm
Surely a little slower and a little slower,
Then one of the old hands drew toward the breast.
The breathing failed; resumed, but waning to silence.
The throat clicked when a breath should have been drawn.
A maze of little wrinkles, that seemed to express
Surprised amusement, played from the hollow eye-pits
Into the beard.

VI

The window was black still.
No cock had cried, nor shiver of dawn troubled the air.
The stale lamp shone and smelled. Ah, what a silence.
She crossed the room and shook Concha. "Get up,
                                        Concha.
He has died. I was alone and have closed his mouth.
Now I'll go out." She thought in the hallway,
"Besides, I am greedy to be caught in Hood's room.
We can but die, what's that. Where did this come from?"
She whispered, staring at the candle she held
Without a memory of having found nor lighted it.
She opened Hood's door and shut it behind her.

                                        "He has died!"
No answer. Then Fera felt the tears in her eyes
Dried up with fear. "You haven't gone? Are you here Hood?"
She saw him lifting his face from the shadows like a sea-lion from
      the wave. "I dreaded
You'd slip away from here in my night. It is finished and I
Alone was by him, your father's flitch of dark meat snored
      in a corner. He has died. All the wild mind

And jagged attempts are sealed over." Her voice lifted and failed,
    he saw her sleep-walker face
Candle-lighted from below, the shadow of the chin covering
    the mouth and of the cheek-bones the eyes
To make it the mask of a strained ecstasy, strained fleshless
    almost. Herself was wondering what sacred fear
Restrained her, she'd meant to go touch, but here desire
    at the height burned crystal-separate. He said, staring:
"Have you called my father? I'll dress and come, what can I do?"
    "Do you think I will call," she said quietly,
"Cawdor?" She stopped and said: "Death is no terror, I have
    just left there. Is there anything possible to fear
And not take what we want, openly with both hands? I have
    been unhappy but that was foolish
For now I know that whatever bent this world around us, whether
    it was God or whether it was blind
Chance piled on chance as blind as my father,
Is perfectly good, we're given a dollar of life to gamble against
    a dollar's worth of desire
And if we sin we have both but losers lose nothing,
Oh, nothing, how are they worse off than my father, or a stone
    in the field? Why, Hood, do you sleep naked?"
She asked him, seeing the candle's gleam on the arm and shoulder.
    "I brought no night-clothes with me," he sullenly
Answered, "I didn't expect people at night. What do you want?"
    "Nothing. Your breast's more smooth
Than rubbed marble, no hair like other men in the groove
    between the muscles, it is like a girl's
Except the hardness and the flat strength. No, why do you cover
    it, why may I not look down with my eyes?
I'd not hide mine. No doubt I'll soon die,
And happy if I could earn that marble to be my gravestone.
    You might cut letters in it. I know
It never would bleed, it would cut hard. *Fera Martial* you'd carve,
    the letters of a saved name,

Why should they fall like grains of sand and be lost forever
On the monstrous beach? But while I breathe I have to come
    back and beat against it, that stone, for nothing,
Wave after wave, a broken-winged bird
Wave after wave beats to death on the cliff. Her blood
    in the foam. If I were another man's wife
And not Cawdor's you'd pity me." "Being what you are," he
    answered: he rose in the bed angrily, her eyes
Took hold like hands upon the beautiful bent shoulders plated
    from the bone with visible power
Long ridges lifting the smooth skin, the hunter slenderness
    and strength: "being what you are you will gather
The shame back on your mind and kill it. We've not been made
    to touch what we would loathe ourselves for
To the last drop." She said "What were you saying? Do you think
    I should be shameless as a man making
Love to reluctance, the man to you for a woman, if I had time,
    if you were not going to-morrow?
If I just had time, I'd use a woman's cunning manners,
    the cat patience and watchfulness: but shame
Dies on the precipice-lip." "I hear them stirring in the house,"
he answered. "You lie, Hood. You hear nothing.
This little room on the north is separate and makes no sound,
    your father used to visit his thing here,
You children slept and heard nothing. You fear him of course.
    I can remember having feared something . . ..
That's long ago. I forget what. Look at me once,
Stone eyes am I too horrible to look at? If I've no beauty
    at all, I have more than Concha had
When she was more fawn than sow, in her lean years, did your
    father avoid her? I must have done something
In ignorance, to make you hate me. If I could help it, would I
    come
Fresh from the death of the one life I have loved to make myself

Your fool and tell you I am shameless, if I could help it? Oh that's
    the misery: you look at me and see death,
I am dressed in death instead of a dress, I have drunk death
    for days, makes me repulsive enough,
No wonder, but you too Hood
Will drink it sometime for all your loathing, there
    are two of us here
Shall not escape.

                    Oh, but we shall though, if you are willing.
    There is one clean way. We'll not take anything
Of Cawdor's, I have two horses of my own. And you can feed
    us with the rifle. Only to ride beside you
Is all I want. But I would waken your soul and your eyes,
    I could teach you joy.

                    I know that you love
Liberty, I'd never touch your liberty. Oh, let me ride beside
    you a week, then you could leave me.
I'd be your . . . whatever you want, but you could have other
    women. That wouldn't kill me; but not to be with you
Is death in torture." Her hope died of his look. "I know we came
    from the fire only to fail,
Fail, fail, it's bred in the blood. But," she cried suddenly, "you
    lie when you look like that. The flesh of my body
Is nothing in my longing. What you think I want
Will be pure dust after hundreds of years and something from
    me be crying to something from you
High up in the air."

                    She heard the door open behind her, she
    turned on the door. Cawdor had come.
She cried "Have you waked at last? You sleep like logs,
    you and your son. He has died. I can wake nobody.

I banged your door, but this one was unlatched and when
    I knocked it flew open. Yet I can't wake him.
Is it decent to leave me alone with the sow Concha
    in the pit of sorrow?" His confused violent eyes
Moved and shunned hers and worked the room, with the ancient
    look of men spying for their own dishonor
As if it were a lost jewel. "How long ago did you knock? I have
    been awake." "What do I know
Of time? He has died." She watched him tremble, controlling
    with more violence the violence in him; and he said:
"I know he has died. I came from that room." Then Fera, knowing
    That Hood looked like a boy caught in a crime but herself like
    innocence: "How did you dare to go in?
Oh yes, the dead never stand up. But how did you dare?
    You never once hid your contempt
While he was living. You came and cursed him because
    our cow died in the creek. Did he want it to die?
Then what have you done just now, spat in his face? I was not there,
    he lay at your mercy." She felt
Her knees failing, and a sharp languor
Melt through her body; she saw the candle-flame (she had set
    the candle on the little table) circling
In a short orbit, and Cawdor's face waver, strange heavy face with
    the drooping brows and confused eyes,
Said something heavily, unheard, and Fera answered:
    "Certainly I could have gone in and called you, but I
Was looking about the house for someone that loved him. You were
    one of the hunters that hunted him down.
I thought that Hood . . . but no, did he care? I couldn't awake
    him. This flesh will harden, I'll be stone too
And not again go hot and wanting pity in a desert of stones.
    But you . . . you . . . that old blind man
Whom you despised, he lived in the house among you a hawk
    in a mole-hill. And now he's flown up. Oh, death

Is over life like heaven over deep hell." She saw Michal
   in the door. "You're here too, Michal?
My father has died. *You* loved him."

                              She said in the hallway,
"Are you well, Michal? I'm not; but when I slept
A snatch of the early night I dreamed about you.
You wrapped yourself in the mountain-lion skin
That Hood gave me, and Jesus Acanna shot you for a lion."

VII

Cawdor remained behind in the room,
But Hood pretended to have been asleep and hardly
Awakened yet. Certainly he'd not betray
The flaming-minded girl his own simplicity
Imagined a little mad in her sorrow. He answered
Safe questions, but the more his intent was innocent
The more his looks tasted of guilt. And Cawdor:
"When are you going?" "To-day." "That's it? By God
You'll wait until the old blind man is buried.
What did she call you for,
Yesterday in the rain?" "She said her father
Was conscious, but when I came he was not conscious."
"Well, he's not now," he answered, his brows drooping
Between the dawn and the candle. Dawn had begun,
And Cawdor's face between the pale window
And the small flame was gray and yellow. "Get dressed," he said.
He turned to go, and turned back. "You were such friends
With that old man, you'll not go till he's buried."

He went and found Fera, in the room with the dead.
But seeing her bloodless face, and the great eyes
Vacant and gray, he grew somberly ashamed
Of having thought her passion was more than grief.
He had meant to charge Concha to watch her
While Hood remained in the house. He forgot that, he spoke
Tenderly, and persuaded Fera to leave
Concha to watch the dead, and herself rest
In her own room. Michal would sit beside her
All morning if she were lonely. "And Hood," he said,
Spying on her face even against his own will,
"Wanted to go to-day, I told him to wait.
Why did you call him, yesterday in the rain?"
"Yesterday?" "You came in the rain." "If that was yesterday:
Our nights have grown long. I think my father called him,
(My father was then alive) wishing to talk
Of the Klamath country. He too had travelled. He despised
     people
Who are toad-stools of one place." "Did they talk long?"
"I can't remember. You know: now he has died.
Now the long-laboring mind has come to a rest.
I am tired too. You don't think that the mind
Goes working on? That would be pitiful. He failed in everything.
After we fail our minds go working under the ground, digging,
     digging . . . we talk to someone,
The mind's not there but digging around its failure. That would
     be dreadful, if even while he lies dead
The painful mind's digging away . . .." Cawdor for pity
Of the paper-white face shrunk small at dawn
Forebore then, he folded his doubts like a man folding
A live coal in his hand.

                    Fera returned
To her father's room; she said, "Concha, go down to breakfast.
     Michal,

Leave me alone for God's sake." Being left alone she knelt
    by the bed: "In that dim world, in that
Dim world, in that dim world, father? . . . there's nothing.
    I am between the teeth still but you are not troubled.
If only you could *feel* the salvation."

                                    She was mistaken. Sleep
    and delirium are full of dreams;
The locked-up coma had trailed its clue of dream across
    the crippled passages; now death continued
Unbroken the delusions of the shadow before. If these had been
    relative to any movement outside
They'd have grown slower as the life ebbed and stagnated
    as it ceased, but the only measure of the dream's
Time was the dreamer, who geared in the same change could feel
    none; in his private dream, out of the pulses
Of breath and blood, as every dreamer is out of the hour-notched
    arch of the sky. The brain growing cold
The dream hung in suspense and no one knew that it did. Gently
    with delicate mindless fingers
Decomposition began to pick and caress the unstable chemistry
Of the cells of the brain; Oh very gently, as the first weak breath
    of wind in a wood: the storm is still far,
The leaves are stirred faintly to a gentle whispering: the nerve-cells,
    by what would soon destroy them, were stirred
To a gentle whispering. Or one might say the brain began
    to glow, with its own light, in the starless
Darkness under the dead bone sky; like bits of rotting wood
    on the floor of the night forest
Warm rains have soaked, you see them beside the path shine like
    vague eyes. So gently the dead man's brain
Glowing by itself made and enjoyed its dream.

                                    The nights of many
    years before this time

He had been dreaming the sweetness of death, as a starved
    man dreams bread, but now decomposition
Reversed the chemistry; who had adored in sleep under so many
    disguises the dark redeemer
In death across a thousand metaphors of form and action celebrated
    life. Whatever he had wanted
To do or become was now accomplished, each bud that had been
    nipped and fallen grew out to a branch,
Sparks of desire forty years quenched flamed up fulfilment.
Out of time, undistracted by the nudging pulse-beat, perfectly
    real to itself being insulated
From all touch of reality the dream triumphed, building from
    past experience present paradise
More intense as the decay quickened, but ever more primitive
    as it proceeded, until the ecstasy
Soared through a flighty carnival of wines and women to the
    simple delight of eating flesh, and tended
Even higher, to an unconditional delight. But then the
    interconnections between the groups of the brain
Failing, the dreamer and the dream split into multitude.
    Soon the altered cells became unfit to express
Any human or at all describable form of consciousness.

                          Pain
    and pleasure are not to be thought
Important enough to require balancing: these flashes
    of post-mortal felicity by mindless decay
Played on the breaking harp by no means countervalued
    the excess of previous pain. Such discords
In the passionate terms of human experience are not resolved,
    nor worth it.

          The ecstasy in its timelessness
Resembled the eternal heaven of the Christian myth, but actually
    the nerve-pulp as organ of pleasure

Was played to pieces in a few hours, before the day's end.
    Afterwards it entered importance again
Through worms and flesh-dissolving bacteria. The personal show
    was over, the mountain earnest continued
In the earth and air.

                    But Fera in her false earnestness
Of passionate life knelt by the bed weeping.
She ceased when Michal returned. Later in the morning
She sent Michal to look for Hood and ask him
Whether he would surely stay as Cawdor had said
Until they buried her father. "Tell him to come
Himself and tell me." Michal came back: "He said
That he was not able to come; but he would stay."
At noon she saw him. She dressed and went to the table,
Where Cawdor sat and watched them. Hood shunned her eyes;
She too was silent.

                    In the afternoon Cawdor came up
And said "The doctor has come." "Why Michal," she said,
    "but that's a pity.
Came all the sloppy way for nothing, the doctor." "No," Cawdor
    said. "I want you to see him, Fera.
You are not well." She went and saw him, in her father's room,
    where Concha with some childhood-surviving
Belief in magic had set two ritual candles burning
    by the bed of death. The doctor hastily
Covered the face, the candle-flames went over in the wind
    of the cloth. Fera stood quietly and said
She had no illness, and her father was dead. "I'm sorry you've
    come so far for nothing." "Oh, well," he answered
"The coast's beautiful after the rain. I'll have the drive."
"Like this old man," she said, "and the other
Millions that are born and die; come all the sloppy
    way for nothing and turn about and go back.

They have the drive." The young doctor stared; and Cawdor
   angrily
Wire-lipped like one who hides a living coal
In the clenched hand: "What more do you want?"
   "Oh," she answered,
"I'm not like that"; and went out.

                              After the doctor had gone
She vomited, and became so weak afterwards
That Michal must call Concha to help undress her.
After another spasm of sickness her dream
Was like a stone's; until Cawdor awakened her
In the night, coming to bed. She lay rigid
And saw the fiery cataracts of her mind
Pour all night long. Before the cock crew dawn
Sea-lions began barking and coughing far off
In the hollow ocean; but one screamed out like torture
And bubbled under the water. Then Fera rose
With thief motions. Cawdor awoke and feigned sleep.
She dressed in the dark and left the room, and Cawdor
Followed silently, the black blood in his throat
Stood like a knotted rope. She entered, however,
Her father's room.

                       She was not surprised, no one was there
And Concha's candles had died. She fingered the dark
To find her father, the body like a board, the sheeted face,
And sat beside the bed waiting for dawn.
Cawdor, returned to his room, left the door open
To hear the hallway; he dressed, and waiting for dawn
Now the first time knew clearly for what reason
He had made Hood stay: that he might watch and know them,
What they had . . . whether they had . . . but that was insane:
One of the vile fancies men suffer

44

When they are too old for their wives. She in her grief?
He had not the faculty common to slighter minds
Of seeing his own baseness with a smile. When Hood had passed
The creaking hallway and gone down-stairs, and the other
Not moved an inch, watching her quiet dead,
Cawdor was cured of the indulgence jealousy,
He'd not be a spy again.

     But Fera had heard
Hood pass; she knew Cawdor was watching; she thought
That likely enough Hood had risen before dawn
To leave the canyon forever. She sat like a stone
Turning over the pages of death in her mind,
Deep water, sharp steel, poisons, they keep in the stable
To wash the wounds of horses . . ..

  VIII

Hood coming in to breakfast from the fragrant light
Before sunrise, had set his rifle in the corner by the door.
George Cawdor left the table and going out-doors
Stopped at the door and took the rifle in his hands
Out of mere idleness. Hood sharply: "Mine. Put it down!"
He, nettled, carried it with him to the next room,
There opened the outer door and lined the sights
With a red lichen-fleck on a dead cypress twig.
Hood came behind him and angrily touched his shoulder,
Reaching across his arm for the rifle; then George,
Who had meant to tease him and give it back in a moment,
Remembered a grudge and fired. The sharp noise rang
Through the open house like a hammer-blow on a barrel.

Hood, in the shock of his anger, standing too near
To strike, struck with his elbow in the notch of the ribs,
His hands to the rifle. George groaned, yet half in sport still
Wrestled with him in the doorway.

                              Hood, not his mind,
But his mind's eye, the moment of his elbow striking
The muscle over the heart, remembered his dream of the night.
A dream he had often before suffered. (This came to his mind
      later, not now; later, when he thought
There is something within us knows our fates from the first,
      our ends from the very fountain; and we in our nights
May overhear its knowledge by accident, all to no purpose,
      it never warns us enough, it never
Cares to be understood, it has no benevolence but only
      knowledge.) He struggled in his dream's twilight
High on the dreadful verge of a cliff with one who hated him
And was more powerful; the man had pale-flaming gray eyes,
      it was the wind blowing from the eyes,
As a wind blew from Fera's, that forced him to the fall
Screaming, for in a dream one has no courage nor self-command
      but only effeminate emotions,
He hung screaming by a brittle laurel-bush
That starved in a crack of the rock. From that he had waked
      in terror. He had lain and thought, if Fera should come
But yet once more pleading for love, he would yield, he would
      do what she wanted . . . but soon that sea-lion shrieking
From the hollow ocean thoroughly awaked him, his mind stepped
      over the weakness, even rubbed it from memory.
What came to him now was only the earlier dream
Mixed with its rage of fear, so that he used
No temperance in the strife with his brother but struck
The next blow with his fist shortened to the mouth,
Felt lips on teeth. They swayed in the gape of the door,

46

Hood the aggressor but George the heavier, entwined like
    serpents,
The gray steel rifle-barrel between their bodies
Appeared a lance on which both struggled impaled.
For still they held it heedfully the muzzle outward
Against the sky through the door.

                                Hood felt a hand
Close on his shoulder like the jaws of a horse
And force him apart from the other, he twisted himself
Without a mind and fought it without knowing whom
He fought with, then a power struck his loins and the hand
Snapped him over. He fell, yet with limbs gathered
Came up as he struck the floor, but even in the crouch
His mind returned. He saw his father, the old man
Still stronger than both his sons, darkening above him;
And George rigid against the wall, blue-faced
Beyond the light of the door; but in the light,
Behind Cawdor, Michal with pitiful eyes.
He said, "Give me the rifle." George, who still held it,
Sucked his cut lip and gave the rifle to Cawdor;
Then Hood rose and stood trembling.

                                But Fera on the stair behind
    them:
She had heard the shot and come down half way: "What have
    you killed," she said, "the mountain-lion? You snapping
    foxes
What meat will you take and be quiet a little? Better than you
Lies quiet up here." But why did her voice ring rather with
    joy than anger? "You deafen the ears of the dead.
Not one of you there is worthy to wash the dead man's body."
    She approached the foot of the stair; her face

Was white with joy. "Poor Hood, has he hurt you? I saw him pluck
you off with two fingers, a beetle from a bread-crumb.
It's lucky for them they'd taken your gun away from you." Cawdor
said somberly, "What do you want here? The boys
Have played the fool, but you can be quiet." "And George,"
she answered, "his mouth is bleeding. What dreams have
stirred you
To make you fight like weasels before the sun has got up? I am a
woman by death left lonely
In a cage of weasels: but I'll have my will: quarrel your hearts
out."
Then Cawdor turned to Hood and gave him the rifle,
And said to George: "I'm going to the hill with Hood
And mark a place for the grave. Get down some redwood
From the shop loft, the twelve-inch planks, when I come down
I'll scribe them for you. And sticks of two-by-four
To nail to at the chest corners." Fera cried "What a burial.
A weasel coffin-maker and another weasel
To dig the grave, a man buried by weasels."
Cawdor said heavily, "Come Hood." And Fera, "The gun too?
Be careful after the grave's dug, I wouldn't trust him."
He turned in the door: "By God I am very patient with you
For your trouble's sake, but the rope frays."

They had gone and Fera said, "What would he do,
Beat me perhaps? He meant to threaten me, Michal?
The man is a little crazy do you think, Michal?"
She walked in the room undoing the dark braids of her hair.
"Why should he blame me for what I say? Blame God,
If there were any.
Your father is old enough to know that nobody
Since the world's birth ever said or did anything
Except from bitter need, except from bitter need.
        How old are you Michal?"

"Fifteen," she said. "Dear, please . . .." "Oh, you'll soon come
    to it.
I am better than you all, that is my sorrow.
What you think is not true." She returned up-stairs
To the still room where one window was blinded
But the other one ached with rose-white light from clouds,
And nothing breathed on the bed.

                              But Michal hasted
And went up the hill to look to her caged eagle.
Hood and her father, she feared, would have to move
The cage, to make room for the grave.

                              She returned and heard
A soft roaring in the kitchen of the house.
"Why have you got the stove roaring, Ilaria?"
"She want hot water," Ilaria Acanna answered,
"She put the boilers over and open the drafts,
I pile in wood." Fera came down. "Not boiling, not yet?
Put in more oak. Oh, are you there Michal?
Common water is fair enough to bathe in
At common times, but now. Let's look out-of-doors.
I want it hot, there are certain stains. Come on.
We'll be back when it's hot." In the wind out-doors
She trembled and said "The world changes so fast,
Where shall we go, to the shore?" Passing the work-shop
Beside the stable they heard a rhythmic noise
Of two harsh notes alternate on a stroke of silence.
Fera stopped dizzily still, and after a moment:
"Although it sounded like my father's breathing,
The days before he died, I'm not fooled, Michal.
A weasel," she said, "gnawing wood. Don't be afraid."
She entered. George lifted his dark eyes
From the saw-cut in the wine-colored redwood planks,

And Fera: "Oh, have you planed them too? That's kind.
The shavings are very fragrant.
How long will these planks last in their dark place
Before they rot and the earth fills them, ten years?"
"These never will rot." "Oh, that's a story. Not redwood even.
There's nothing under the sun but crumbles at last,
That's known and proved. . . . Where's the other weasel?"
    He looked
Morosely into her face and saw that her eyes
Gazed past him toward the skin of the mountain-lion
That Hood had given her. It was nailed wide and flat
In the gable-end, to dry, the flesh side outward,
Smeared with alum and salt. "Your brother weasel,"
She said, "Hood, Hood. The one that nibbled your lip.
How it is swollen." Not George but Michal answered
That Hood was up on the hill; "they had to move
My eagle's cage." Fera looked up at the lion-skin:
"I'll take that, George, that's mine." "Hm, the raw skin?"
"No matter," she said, "get it down. It's for my father.
What else have we got to give him? I'll wrap him in it
To lie like a Roman among the pale people.
. . . On your fine planks!" "You're more of a child than Michal,"
He said compassionately. "When you said *child*,
Your face," she answered, "softened I thought.
It's not like Hood's." He climbed up by the work-bench and drew
    the tacks,
She stood under him to take the skin, Michal beside her. The scene
    in the dim work-shop gable-end
Wakes a sunk chord in the mind . . . the scene is a descent from
    the cross. The man clambering and drawing
The tyrannous nails from the pierced paws; the sorrowful women
    standing below to receive the relic,
Heavy-hanging spoil of the lonely hunter whom hunters
Rejoice to kill: . . . that Image-maker, its drift of metaphors.
George freed the skin, Fera raised hands to take it.

Her small hard pale-brown hands astonished him, so pale
　　and alive,
Folding the tawny rawhide into a bundle.
"Where's Cawdor," she said, "your father: on the hill with
　　Hood?"
He had gone up to Box Canyon with Dante Vitello,
Michal answered. And Fera: "Oh, but how hard it is.
Perhaps it could be oiled? It is like a board.
I'll take it to him." But Michal remained with George,
Tired of her restlessness, and afraid of her eyes.

Fera went up carrying the skin in her arms
And took it into the house. Ilaria Acanna
Came out to meet her. "Your water's boiling." "Well,
　　let it stand."
She laid, in the still room-up-stairs, the hard gift
Over her father's body. "Oh, that looks horrible,"
She cried shuddering and twitched it off. To hide it from sight
She forced it into the wardrobe against the wall,
The one she had moved to block the broken window
In the wild time of storm. She stood and whispered to herself,
And eyed the bed; then she returned out-doors,
And up the hill to the grave, in the oak's earth-bench
Above the house. The pit was waist-deep already,
And Hood was in the pit lifting the pick-axe
Between the mounds of wet red earth and cut roots.
Acanna leaned on a shovel above the pit-mouth.
For lack of room they had dug west of the oak;
The two old graves lay east. The eagle's cage
Was moved a few feet farther west; Hood labored
Between the cage and the oak. Jesus Acanna
From under the low cloud of the oak-boughs, his opaque eyes
And Indian silence watched Fera come up the hill,
But the eagle from the cage watched Hood labor; the one

With dark indifference, the other
With dark distrust, it had watched all the grave-digging.

Fera stood among the cut roots and said,
Lifting her hand to her face: "I was worn out yesterday
With not sleeping; forgive me for foolish words.
I came up here to tell you: for I suppose
You'll go away to-night or to-morrow morning.
Well, I am taught.
I wish that when you go you'd take for a gift
One of my white ponies, they'll have to bear being parted.
Good-bye. Live freely but not recklessly. The unhappy old man
For whom you are digging the hole, lost by that.
He never could learn that we have to live like people in a web
    of knives, we mustn't reach out our hands
Or we get them gashed." Hood gazing up from the grave:
    "I'm sorry. Yes, early in the morning." He glanced
    at Acanna
And said, "One thing I know, I shan't find loveliness in another
    canyon, like yours and Michal's." She turned
Away, saying "That's no help," and seemed about to go down;
    but again turning: "I meant to gather
Some branches of mountain laurel. There are no flowers
This time of year. But I have no knife. It shouldn't be all like
    a dog's burial." "I'll cut some for you."
He climbed out of the grave and said to Acanna: "I'll soon
    be back. If you strike rock at this end,
Level off the floor." Fera pointed with her hand trembling:
    "The tree's in the gap behind the oak-trees.
It's farther but the leaves are much fresher. Indeed he deserves
    laurel, his mind had wings and magnificence
One dash of common cunning would have made famous.
    And died a cow's death. You and I, if we can bear
The knocks and abominations of fortune for fifty years yet, have
    as much to hope for. Don't come. I'm not

A cheerful companion. Lend me the knife."
He thought she had better not be trusted alone with it,
The mind she was in,
And went beside her, above the older graves,
He felt his knees trembling. Across the steep slope
To the far oaks. Dark aboriginal eyes,
The Indian's and the coast-range eagle's, like eyes
Of this dark earth watching our alien blood
Pass and perform its vanities, watched them to the far oaks.
But after the oaks had hidden them Acanna
Covetously examined the hunter's rifle
Left behind, leaning against the lichened fence
Of the older graves. It was very desirable. He sighed
And set it back in its place.

              Fera in the lonely
Oak-shielded shadow under the polished laurel-leaves: "Before
      you came
I used to come here," she caught her quivering under lip with
      the teeth to keep it quiet, "for solitude.
Here I was sure no one would come, not even the deer, not a bird;
      safer than a locked room.
Those days I had no traitor in my own heart, and would gather
      my spirit here
To endure old men.

              That I have to die
Is nothing important: though it's been pitied sometimes when
      people are young: but to die in hell. I've lived
Some days of it; it burns; how I'd have laughed
Last year to think of anyone taken captive by love. A girl imagines
      all sorts of things
When she lives lonely but this was never . . .. Who knows what
      the dead feel, and it is frightful to think
That after I have gone down and stilled myself in the hissing
      ocean: roll, roll on the weed: this hunger

Might not be stilled, this fire nor this thirst . . .
For how can anyone be sure that death is a sleep? I've never
 found the little garden-flower temperance
In the forest of the acts of God . . . . Oh no, all's forever there,
 all wild and monstrous
Outside the garden: long after the white body beats to bone
 on the rock-teeth the unfed spirit
Will go screaming with pain along the flash of the foam, gnawing
 for its famine a wrist of shadow,
Torture by the sea, screaming your name. I know these things.
 I am not one of the careful spirits
That trot a mile and then stand."

        He had bared his knife-blade
 to cut the bough, enduring her voice, but Fera
Caught the raised wrist. "Let it be. We have no right. The trees
 are decent, but we! A redwood cut
To make the coffin, an oak's roots for the grave: some
 day the coast will lose patience and dip
And be clean. Ah. Is it men you love?
You are girl-hearted, that makes you ice to me? What do you love?
 What horror of emptiness
Is in you to make you love nothing? Or only the deer and the wild
 feet of the mountain and follow them
As men do women. Yet you could dip that little knife-blade
 in me for pleasure, I'd not cry out
More than a shot deer, but I will never leave you
Until you quiet me." She saw that his face was gray and strained
 as a spent runner beaten at the goal.
"Will you kiss me, once, you are going away in a moment
 forever? What do you owe Cawdor, what price
Of kindness bought you? This morning it was: he struck
 you and flung you on the ground: you liked that?"
He gathered his strength

And turned himself to be gone. She caught him and clung,
And fallen to her knees when he moved outward, "I swear by God,"
    she said, "I will tell him that you have taken me
Against my will, if you go from here before I have spoken. You'll
    not be hurt, Hood, you'll be far off,
And what he can do to *me* is no matter." He said "You have
    gone mad. Stand up. I will listen." But she
Feeling at last for the first time some shadow of a power
To hold and move him would not speak nor stand up, but crouched
    at his feet to enjoy it. At length she lifted
Wide staring eyes and fever-stained face. "I am very happy.
    I don't know what has told me: some movement
Or quietness of yours." She embraced his thighs, kneeling before
    him, he felt her breasts against them, her head
Nuzzling his body, he felt with his hand the fire of her throat,
    "Nothing," he said,
"Is worse nor more vile than what we are doing." "What? With
    a little . . . sin if you call it . . . kill a great misery?
No one," she thought, "ever tastes triumph
Until the mouth is rinsed with despair." She sobbed "I have
    found you." But when he had dropped the knife at the tree's
    root
To free his hand, and lay by her side on the drifted fall of the crisp
    oak-leaves and curled brown laurel-leaves,
Then she who had wooed began to resist him, to lengthen
    pleasure. "I have lighted the fire, let me warm
    my hands at it
Before we are burned." The face of her exultation was hateful
    to him. He thought of the knife in the leaves
And caught it toward him and struck the point of the blade into
    the muscle of his thigh. He felt no pain
A moment, and then a lightning of pain, and in the lit clearance:
    "I am not your dog yet," he said easily,
"I am not your thing." He felt her body shudder and turn stone
    above him. "What have you done?" "A half inch

55

Into the blood," he answered, "I am better." He stood
    up. "You will be grateful
To-morrow, for now we can live and not be ashamed. What sort
    of life would have been left us?" "No life
Is left us," she said from a loose throat.
"This mountain is dry." She stood and whispered "I won't
    do anything mean or troublesome. I pitied my father's
Failures from the heart, but then quietness came." Her teeth
    chattered together, she said "I will now go down
If you will let me?" He followed, limping from the Attis-gesture,
Outside the oaks and watched her creep toward the house.
The blood gliding by his knee he rubbed a handful of earth
Against the stain in the cloth to embrown the color.
And went faintly to the work he had left.

IX

                                                  Michal
Came up after a time with meat for the eagle.
While she fed it they had sunk the grave though shallow
To the hard rock and ceased. "Have you seen Fera
Lately?" Hood asked, "she was here wanting some greens
Because there are no flowers, but seemed to be taken sick
With grief and went down." "No. I was into the house
But not up-stairs." "We'd better see how she is.
Bring down the axe and pick-axe," he said to Acanna,
"But leave the spades." He stepped short, to conceal
His lameness. Michal asked him, "What's the long stain?"
"Sap from the oak-roots, they're full of water."

                                                  They
    looked for Fera
All over the house and found her lying on the floor

56

The far side of her father's bed. Hood watched in terror
While Michal touched; he thought she had killed herself.
He had held an obscure panic by force a prisoner
All day but now it was worse, it was a wish to be gone,
"There's nothing I wouldn't give to have gone yesterday.
Oh, pitiful child." She moved; she was not self-slain. She rose
To Michal's tugging hands and was led to bed
In her own room, hanging back but in silence.
Toward evening she dressed herself with Concha helping
In the blue serge that was the darkest she had,
And went with the others up the hill to the burial.

A man at each corner carried the oblong box,
Cawdor and his sons and Dante Vitello. But Hood was lame,
And when his left foot slipped on a stone his right
Failed with the weight. The stiff unseasonable
Calla lilies that Michal had found by water
Fell down the tilted lid; she gathered them up,
And when the box was lowered into its place
Dropped them upon it. Jesus Acanna had brought
The cords to use for lowering. All was done awkwardly
By shame-faced people, and the eagle watched from the cage.
The coffin grounding like a shored boat, the daughter
Of the tired passenger sighed, she leaned in the blindness
Of sand-gray eyes behind Michal toward Hood.
Her hand touched his, he trembled and stepped aside
Beyond Concha Rosas. Then Fera pressed her knuckles
        to her mouth
And went down the hill; the others remained.

Because of the dug earth heaped at the oak's foot
They were all standing on the west side the grave
Or at either end, a curious group, Cawdor's gray head the tallest,
Nine, to count Concha's child,

Intent, ill at ease, like bewildered cattle nosing one fallen.
Not one of them, now that Fera was gone,
Had any more than generic relation to the dead; they were merely
    man contemplating man's end,
Feeling some want of ceremony.

                              The sky had been overcast;
        between the ocean and the cloud
Was an inch slit, through which the sun broke suddenly at setting,
    only a fraction of his passing face,
But shone up the hill from the low sea's rim a reddening fire from
    a pit. The shadows of the still people
Lay like a bundle of rods, over the shallow grave, up the red
    mound of earth, and upward
The mass of the oak; beyond them another shadow,
Broad, startling and rectilinear, was laid from the eagle's cage;
    nine slender human shadows and one
Of another nature.

        Jesus Acanna
Saw something like a jewel gleam in the rays
On the heap of surface earth at his feet; he stooped
And picked it up; a knife-edged flake of wrought
Chalcedony, the smooth fracture was pleasant to feel.
He stood and fondled it with his fingers, not mindful
That his own people had chipped it out and used it
To scrape a hide in their dawn or meat from a shell.

Then Cawdor made a clearing noise in his throat
And said in heavy embarrassment: "We know nothing
    of God, but we in our turn shall discover death.
It might be good to stand quietly a moment, before we fill
    in the dirt, and so if anyone
Is used to praying"—he looked at Concha and Ilaria—"might say it
    in their minds." They stood with their eyes lowered,

And Cawdor took up a shovel and said impatiently
"Let us fill in." The sun was gone under the wine-colored ocean,
    then the deep west fountained
Unanticipated magnificences of soaring rose and heavy purple,
    atmospheres of flame-shot
Color played like a mountain surf, over the abrupt coast,
    up the austere hills,
On the women talking, on the men's bent forms filling the grave,
    on the oak, on the eagle's prison, one glory
Without significance pervaded the world.

                                        Fera had gone down
To the emptied room in the vacant house to do
What she had imagined in the afternoon. In the pain of her mind
Nothing appeared fantastic; she had thought of a way
To trick death from the hands that refused life.
From Hood's own hands. She'd not be forgotten. She drew
The mountain-lion skin from where it was crumpled away,
And clothed herself in it, the narrow shoulders
Over her shoulders, the head over her head.
She bound it with bits of string, and smoothed the wrinkles.
It would fool a hunter in the twilight; only her face
Must be turned from him. She fled from the house and hid
In the oaks against the hill, not far from the door.
The rosy light had waned from the cloud, wilderness-hearted
Twilight was here, embrowning the leaves and earth.
Concha and Ilaria and Concha's child came talking
And entered the house; kitchen windows were lighted.
The others delayed. Blue smoke began to veil out
And be fragrant among the leaves. She crouched in the oak-bush,
As every evening the wild lives of the mountain
Come down and lie watching by lonely houses.

Hood, when they took the redwood box to the house,
Had left his rifle in the stable, he came with Michal,

Having fetched it. They walked mournfully together,
For this was their last evening, he'd leave at dawn
For the free north. But nothing remained to say;
And through their silence, drawing near the house-door, Michal
Heard the stiff oak-leaves move, she looked and perceived
A life among them, laying her hand on his arm
She pointed with the other hand. The head and slant shoulder
And half the side unsheathed themselves from the oak,
The hindquarters were hidden. The long beast lifted
On straightened fore-legs and stood quartering away,
The head raised, turned up the canyon. Hood held his fire,
Astonished at it, wasn't it one of the dogs?
Both dogs were splatched with white, the brindle was dead,
No white on this, and light enough yet remained
To show the autumn color and the hair's texture;
Here were the paws that killed the brindle and the calf;
In vain hunted; chance-met.

                But Fera supposed
His weapon was in his room in the house, he'd slip
Into the house to fetch it and she'd have fled
When he returned; hunting alone up the twilight hill
Might he not even now discover a woman
In the beast's hide, pity that woman? Already in her mind
She wavered away from the necessity of death;
If Michal had not been present she might have stood up
And shown . . . .
The stroke that ended her thought was aimed too low.
In the hunter's mind a more deep-chested victim
Stood in the dusk to be slain; what should have transpierced
The heart broke the left arm-bone against the shoulder
And spared the life.

                He knew, as she fell. He seemed to himself
To have known even while he fired. That worm of terror

Strangled his mind so that he kept no memory
Of Cawdor and the others taking her into the house.
He was left in the dark with a bruised face, someone had struck him,
Oh, very justly.

                  He rose and stood reeling
Like a boy whom bad companions have filled with sweetened
Liquor, to make him their evening sport. The yellow
Windows of the house wavered, he fought the sickness
And went in-doors. Someone stared at him passing
Up-stairs; he heard from the door her moaning breath.
Cawdor examined the wound, George held the lamp
Over the naked arm and breast, Concha
Was dipping a sponge: it was the dark clot
Stringing from the red sponge that overcame him.
Cawdor's face, like a rock to break on, turned
To say hoarsely "You bastard, get out of this place,"
And turned back to the wound; terrible face in the lamp-shadow
Black as the blood-clot.

                  He stood outside the door
Half fainting against the wall. Wanted him to go?
Good God, did he want to stay? Michal came whispering:
"You can't do anything here; and I am afraid of father.
Please go. Please go. To-morrow I'll meet you somewhere.
Oh, what can you do here?"

                  While he limped on the stairway
Fera's moan sharpened and became a voice.
He found himself out of doors; the blanket-roll
He had rolled ready to start to-morrow at dawn
Was in his hand. He looked for his rifle
On the ground between the shot and the mark, and stumbled
    over it
After he had failed to find it.

                              The sky had cleared
With its local suddenness, full of nail-sharp stars
And a frosty dust of shining; he went up the dim star-path
By the lone redwood into wide night. His usurped mind
Unheeding itself ran in its track of habit,
So that he went from the oaks as before, upward
The gravelly slope of spoiled granite to the Rock.
He soon gathered dead twigs and kindled a fire
On the dome of the Rock, wishing Michal might see it
And bring him word in the morning. The night had turned
Frostily cold with its cleared sky.

        X

                              Fera's moan became vocal, she
        flapped the hurt arm, the hand
Lying still and hooked, the marbled flesh working between
        the shoulder and the elbow. Michal remembered
Her eagle in the fresh of its wound waving the broken
        flag: another one of Hood's rifle-shots. Cawdor
Gripped the shoulder quiet with his hand, and clinked in the basin
From his right hand the small red splinter of bone he had fished
        from the wound. Fera's eye-lids, that hung
Half open on arcs of opaque white, widened suddenly,
        and fluttered shut, and stood wide open,
The liquid pools of night in the rayed gray rings dilating
        and contracting like little hearts,
Each sparked with a minute image of the lamp above them.
        She tongued her lips and the dry teeth
And moved her head. "This must be life, this hot pain.
Oh, the bad hunter! I fail in everything, like my father." Cawdor
        looked sideways to place in his mind

The strips of a torn sheet laid ready, and smooth straight sticks
   of pinewood kindling fetched from the kitchen;
He pressed a ragful of pungent liquid to the wound's mouths.
   Fera lay quiet, but Michal trembled
To see her lips retract from the teeth, and hear the teeth creaking
   together. Then Fera whispered:
"Horse-liniment. Of course you would. It burns." But Cawdor
   answered: "Hold the lamp, Michal. George, hold
   her quiet."
He gripped with his hands the shoulder and the upper
   arm. Then Fera: "Oh God! Oh no! No . . . no . . .
I'll tell you anything . . . .." The ends of the fracture were heard
   touching; but she writhing her body whipped over
In George's and Concha's hands; Cawdor held without failure
   but her movement baffled him, the ends of bone
Were heard slipping. He shifted his grasp and said to the others,
   "Loose-handed fools. Hold firm." But Fera
Straining her chalky and diminished face, the earth-stain still
   unwashed on her cheek, clear of the pillow:
"Oh, please. Dearest! I'll not hide anything. I'm not to blame."
   His mind was fixed on his work, yet even
While his muscles were setting themselves again her words
 · entered his understanding. His grip relaxed;
He looked at her face, the eyes stared bright terror but the mouth
Attempting a fawning smile: "I'll tell you everything, dearest,
   but don't torture me. I thought I had tasted
Torture before. How little I knew." Her teeth chattered together
   and she said "He forced me. Hood forced me.
He threw me down under the laurel tree
And stopped my mouth with his hand. So that I couldn't be your
   wife any more, darling. But I
Never loved him. I only tried to be killed. Oh, Oh, his face
Is like a nigger's. George, save me! Michal!" He sighed, "You
   lie. Be quiet." "Darling," she pleaded, "I feel

Pain so much more than you understand. I can't *bear* pain? *Bear*
    pain? I am not made like the people
You're used to." He wavered his head as if a fringe hung over
    the eyes, and bent to the wound, but she:
"I only tried to be killed." He muttered, "I don't kill women."
    And Fera: "You'd be so kind. Oh,
But the darkness was sweet." And feeling his hands, "Oh, Concha,"
    she cried, "I've told him everything and yet he'll hurt me.
Dear Concha pray to him for me, he used to love you. And I have
    never been mean to you because of that,
Concha." Then Cawdor suddenly turned to the Indian woman:
    "Is it true, what she says?" But Michal: "No, no,
Her mind," she stammered, "gone wrong. Ah, you coward,
    Fera." "And what part," Cawdor said, "had *you* in the play?
By God, you all . . .. When?" he said hoarsely to Fera. "Before
    he died," she answered, her breath hissing
In little pulses. He gathered his strength and said, "Out, Michal."
    And when she had gone: "Was it in this room,
Or his?" She answered "Under the laurel tree
He threw me down: I was not to blame not to blame more
Than a murdered man is." George said, "She is lying. Her madness
    is fear of pain. She is sick." "Though I've been played
For the fool of the world I know more than that. They make
    lies for pleasure but not
Get killed for pleasure. You sick whore, does it hurt? Here
    is a different bed from the brown leaves
And the panting dog." Her face looking no bigger than a broken
    doll's on the pillow answered: "I knew
You'd kill me, I didn't think torture, why must I suffer alone?
    If I am to blame a little is he
Not rich with blame? He has got away I suppose. I swear
    by God I never consented to him.
It was all violence, violence . . .. Have pity: no pity?
    Sweetheart: I never called you before: Sweetheart,

64

Have mercy on me." He stood as if to go out of the room;
   he was heard breathing, and slowly his hands
Crept to his throat. He turned and came back and said:
   "It is not to punish you.
I must set the bone. You can't stay here and be kept, you'll need
   both arms to live with. I will use all
Gentleness: but you lie still, it will be done in a moment. I'll send
   for the doctor, but when he comes
It will be too swollen perhaps for mending. Indeed I have other
   business. People take pain like bread
When their life needs it. After it is set the ache
Will quiet, you'll sleep."

                    Michal, outside the door,
Heard her screaming and went in; but then she had fainted
And Cawdor worked more easily. He bound the arm
And set the splints, and bound it again, and passed
A leather belt about her body to fasten it
Against her side. He looked then at her face,
The dark lashes lying still, the parted white lips
Pencilled at the borders with fine blue lines,
Meek as a child's after the turn of fever
Folds its weakness in sleep. Concha prepared
To bathe the face, but Cawdor: "Let her alone.
Let her have the poor mercy while it lasts.
Come George, I'll help you saddle. He'll come sooner
For you than another." He spoke quietly, but leaving
The room he walked against the wall by the door
And spread his hands both ways to feel the door-frame
Before he went out. He ran and found Hood's room
Empty, before he went with George to the stable.
"I think it has cleared," he said in the dark, "aren't the stars
   out?"
He saw the red star of Hood's fire on the Rock.

"Take your pick of the horses: I must go back
And warn the women: she will wake in delirium
And strain the bandages loose: I didn't speak of that,
That I remember? That I remember? Good-night,"
He said eagerly. He turned, then George went down
Alone, but Cawdor up the hill to the Rock
As one tortured with thirst toils up the sand-hills
To the known rock spring. When he issued from the oaks
On the ridge of the steep neck of air-crumbled granite
The canyon redwoods were a stain of black shade
In the pit below, the gleam-powdered sky soared
        out of conception,
The starlight vastness and steepness were narrow to him
And no wind breathed. He was like one threading a tunnel
With anguished hunger of the air and light, all the arrows
Of desire strung to their heads on the pale spark
Of day at the end: so all the needs of his life
Hung on the speck of humanity by the red embers
On the rock dome. It heard him, and twitched and stood up.
He made in his mouth and waterless throat the words
"Come down," but no sound issued; he came nearer and said
"What did you steal? Come down." Hood screamed "Keep off,"
The same panic of brainless fear returning,
With a horror of his own cowardice, how could he bear
To run, but how could he bear to stand? He imagined
Fera had died. His very innocence of evil
Made the avenger unbearable, one of those hands
Could break his body, he snatched his rifle and stood
On the other side of the embers and sobbed "Stop there.
By God if you come nearer I'll fire. Keep off your hands.
I'm not hiding, I'll answer the law, not you.
I can't . . .. Keep off. Oh! Oh!" For Cawdor blindly
Came through the fire; Hood with the rifle at his waist
Unshouldered, flung up the muzzle and shot in the air

Over his father's head: at the flash Cawdor
Felt a bright fear, not of death but of dying mocked,
Overreached and outraged, as a fool dies,
Explode on his mind like light breaking on blindness
So that the body leaped and struck while the mind
Astonished with hatred stood still. There had been no choice,
Nor from the first any form of intention.
He saw Hood's body roll away from the fire
Like a thing with no hands; he felt in the knuckles
Of both his hands that both had been bruised on bone,
He saw Hood's body twist on the fall of the dome
Over the precipice and hands like weak flames
Scratch at the starlight rock: then one sharp moment's
Knife-edge a shadow of choice appeared: for all
Passed in a moment: he might have dived prone
And clutched after the hands with his hands: more likely
Gone down the granite slide into the gulf
With the other: but the choice had no consciousness
And in a moment, no choice. There was no cry.
The curving hands scrabbled on the round of the rock
And slipped silently down, into so dreadful a depth
That no sound of the fall: nothing returned:
Mere silence, mere vanishing. Cawdor could hear the water
Whispering below, and saw the redwood forest
A long irregular stain in the starlit gorge-bottom,
But over the round of the rock it was not possible
To see the foot of the Rock. A little steady breeze
Blew curving up over the granite verge
From the night's drift in the chasm.

                                    He turned and walked
Stealthily away, yet firmly, feeling no horror
But only a hollow unbearable sadness. But Hood had earned

The death he had got: not that he'd used violence
In adultery, that was incredible, the woman had lied:
But the crime however invited had no forgiveness,
Not even in death. Women are not responsible;
They are like children, little children grown lewd;
Men must acknowledge justice or their world falls
Piecemeal to dirty decay. Justice had been
Performed. He felt the sapping unbearable sadness
A little lightened, so muttered "Justice. Justice.
Justice": but the third time of saying it the word
Was pithed of meaning and became useless. He had come
Half way to the house and there remembered the things
Left on the Rock. He returned. Only his knowledge
Of what lay at the foot prevented him then
From casting himself down. Nor could he cast the rifle,
The silly rifle that Hood had loved,
For fear of its falling on the poor damned face.
He stood between the blanket-roll and the rifle
Beside a few burnt sticks and scattered red coals
On the bulge of the Rock. "Well, I have killed my son." Whether
    he continued living or quit living,
It would be a pity Michal should know. Quit, because it hurts?
    He thought he was not the make to do that.
His recent real temptation appeared a contemptible flourish
    of play-acting. "Well, I have killed my son.
He needed killing." The woman's story of the rape
    was now believed; it had become needful
To believe her story. "I will take these and bury them with
    him." When he'd again gone under the oaks
He heard one coming up the dark path. A moment of stupid
    horror he dreamed it was Hood coming
To claim the rifle. But Michal, no doubt, Michal. He laid
    the things he carried into the darkness
Of the oaks by the path, and hardened his mind to meet Michal.
    Meet . . . whom? It brushed against the stiff leaves

68

Like something broken that crept and rested. With no terror
   but pity going down in the dark to meet it
He heard it snort and stamp hooves, a stray horse plunged from
   the path. "God damn you," he said and a voice answered
From down the path: "Hood, is that you?" She had been coming
   up to the Rock, and the strayed horse
Drifting ahead. She said "One of the horses: I guess it's gone.
   O Hood, Fera has said
Frightful . . . where are you?" She cried sharply "Who is that?"
   "The things were true," he answered, "all true." He heard
   her
Stop, and he seemed to feel her trembling. "Where's Hood,"
   she said in a moment, trembling, "what have you done?"
"Nothing." He said in his heart "Well: I have killed him?"
   He possessed his voice in quietness and said, "I came
To ask him the truth, and he has confessed. It was all true."
   She sobbed and said "What have you done with him?"
"Nothing," he answered indifferently. "He ran when I came.
   A guilty conscience, Michal. He has done a thing
Never forgiven." He had reached her now; in the starless night
   of the oaks he saw the gleam of her face
Retreating, she moving slowly backward before him. He said
   "Like the scut of a deer." "What?" "When I came
He streaked up the hill into the starlight." "How did you make
   him confess?" "Oh Michal, a guilty conscience.
That does it. You know he wasn't a coward by nature, not
   a damned coward. I saw him run like a rabbit-scut
Between the hill and the stars. Come up to the Rock and call
   him." "I thought I heard a gun-shot," she faltered.
"I was in the house with . . . .. Then I went out." "A gun-shot?
   No. Come up and call him; perhaps he'll come down.
I promise you not to touch him. Come up and call to him, Michal.
   If you call loudly." They climbed to the Rock.
She saw it was vacant, the ends of a few sticks glowed on the stone,
   pale in their ash-crusts. "Hood. Hood,"

She called, and he said "Call louder. He has gone
     far." She answered,
"No, I won't call. I wish never to see him."

Who lay under the sheer below them, his broken shoulders
Bulging his coat in lumps the starlight regarded.
The bone vessel where all the nerves had met
For counsel while they were living, and the acts and thoughts
Been formed, was burst open, its gray and white jellies
Flung on the stones like liquor from a broken flask,
Mixed with some streamers of blood.

                              The vivid consciousness
That waking or dreaming, its twenty years, infallibly
Felt itself unitary, was now divided:
Like the dispersion of a broken hive: the brain-cells
And rent fragments of cells finding
After their communal festival of life particular deaths.
In their deaths they dreamed a moment, the unspent chemistry
Of life resolving its powers; some in the cold star-gleam
Some in the cooling darkness in the crushed skull.
But shine and shade were indifferent to them, their dreams
Determined by temperatures, access of air,
Wetness or drying, as the work of the autolytic
Enzymes of the last hunger hasted or failed.

Yet there appeared, whether by chance or whether
From causes in their common origin and recent union,
A rhythmic sympathy among the particular dreams.
A wave of many minute delicious enjoyments
Would travel across the spilth; then a sad fading
Would follow it, a wave of infinitesimal pains,
And a pause, and the pleasures again. These waves both lessened
In power and slowed in time; the fragments of consciousness
Beginning to lapse out of the frailties of life

70

And enter another condition. The strained peace
Of the rock has no repose, it is wild and shuddering, it travels
In the teeth of locked strains unimaginable paths;
It is full of desire; but the brittle iniquities of pleasure
And pain are not there. These fragments now approached
What they would enter in a moment, the peace of the earth.

XI

When Cawdor had left the house, Concha
At once busied herself to recall to life
The milk-faced bandaged one on the bed, then Michal
Had intervened: "He said to let her alone.
He said to let her have peace." But Concha: "She stay
Fainting too long, she stop breathing, she die."
"I think that would be better." But the Indian woman
Trembling went on, then Michal held up the basin
While the other bathed the pale face, gray jewels of water
Ran down in the hair. There was no response; then Michal
Herself began to be frightened. She knew that her father
Had kept a bottle of whiskey somewhere in the room;
She set the basin on the blue chair and went
Searching on shelves.

                    Concha flung back the sheet
And blanket to bathe the breast. How the hard strap
That held the arm furrowed the flesh of the waist.
The fine-grained clear white skin was beautiful to her;
The coins of rose about the small nipples
Astonished her; hers were as black as the earth; she dipped her head
As if to a flower's fragrance and felt the quiet breasts
She had cooled with water move on her face: Fera
Moaned and then said faintly, "You are blind, father.

Both horses were white." She moved her head on her hair,
Her voice changed: "Do you love me, Concha? You never
    were jealous
I've wondered at you. Where's Cawdor?" Michal returned
And said sullenly: "I've found it, and there's no glass.
She'd better suck from the bottle." But Fera lay
Regardless of her, and dropping her right forearm
Across her breast, explored the splints, and folds
On heavy folds of linen that shelled the shoulder
And the left arm; then with pain-dwindled lips,
"Well," she said, "give it to me. It's time for me now
To taste of my father's friend. Help me sit up, Concha."
She sipped and choked; it spilled on her chin, the burning
    fragrance
Filled all the room. Michal took back the bottle
And said, "Why did you lie? You lied. You lied
Horrible things." Fera, dull-eyed, with racked mouth,
The coughing had hurt her arm: "Not lies. Every word
Faithful as death. I lay between your father and your brother
Like a snake between the rock and the stone.
Give me the bottle, give it back to me Michal.
I have to hush this torment. Your father'll come back.
And beat me with his fists like a wild beast,
He's like a beast in his rages." "Every word's lies.
But if it were true, why did you tell him?" "Because he
    tortured me."
Michal crossed the room to the corner and saw
In the east window high up in the dark pane
A little drop of red light. She pressed her face
Against the glass and cupped it with her two hands
To shut the lamplight away. Hood's waning fire,
Like a red star under the diamond stars.
"I'll go and ask him," she said turning. "He'll tell me
Every last word was a lie." "What did you see, Oh what
    did you see, Michal?"

72

Fera said shaking, "A fire on the Rock? It's only some vaquero
    from inland, Hood wouldn't build one,
Not to-night, not to-night." She answered "I saw nothing.
    I saw the sky and some stars. Concha,
Take care of her, will you. Get her to sleep." As Michal crossed
    to the door a dim noise like a gun-shot
Seemed to be heard, she said "Oh, what was that? Concha:
    you heard it? Listen." But Fera laughing
With an ashen face: "Lived here all her life long
And never has heard a wave slapping the sand
        at the creek-mouth."

                        When she'd gone out, Fera said:
    "Concha,
My father's blindness was crystal to hers. How could she stay
    in the room and let Cawdor go out
To find his prey in the night? Did she know *nothing*? Give
    me the bottle, dear Concha. Dear Concha." She drank,
And said: "I'd no other way to keep him, he was going away.
    Poor hunter. I set a beast on his track
That he's no match for. The gun's no good, boy hunter, you might
    as well toss acorns. Two bulls, Concha,
Fighting by starlight, the young one is gored. Ah: Concha:
One of my loves was locked in the hill by the oak, now the other's
    safe too. Listen: my birthday's to-night.
Has to be kept," she stammered, "I've told no one but you. And
    here's my father's friend to sit up with.
Go down and get two glasses, Concha, and a pitcher of water."
    She called her back from the door. "Concha!
The water in the house is all stale.
Go out to the spring among the calla lilies
And fill the pitcher. Don't hurry, Concha, I'm resting now."

                                            As
    Concha went out Fera stealthily

Undid the belt that locked her arm to her side; when the Indian
   was gone
She passed one-handed the strap through the buckle, the tongue
   thrown back
To let it slide free. She knotted the end of the strap
To the top of the carved bed-post, kneeling on the pillow,
Tightening the knot between her hand and her teeth.
She dropped the collar about her neck, and shuffled her knees
Until they slipped from the mattress. The right arm
Sustained the left one, to ease its pain in the fall.
She could have breathed by standing, but while her mind
Remained she would not, and then was unable.

                                        Concha,
         down-stairs,
Had much to tell Ilaria. Acanna was there too
In the kitchen, and Concha's boy Romano, and Dante
Vitello, the Swiss. All questioned her. She'd forgotten
The water and found the glasses, when little Romano
In his child voice: "Escucha: un raton. —Listen mother,
A mouse in the ceiling." But no one looked up nor down
Until he fetched the gray cat from under the stove
And wanted to take her up-stairs. Concha forbade him,
But listened, and heard the noise in the ceiling change
From a soft stroking to a dull shudder in the wood.
The shudder was Fera's agony; the backs of her feet
Stroking the floor; she hung as if kneeling. But Concha said:
"A trade-rat maybe: no mouse. But I must go up."
The noise had ceased.

                              She screamed in the hallway above
And flung the glasses on the floor. The people below
Stared at each other. Her cries were timed, rhythmic,
Mechanical, like a ground-squirrel's when he sits up
Beside his burrow and watches a dog hunting

On the other side of the fence. At length Acanna
Ran to the stair, the others followed, and little Romano
With gray puss in his arms. They looked past Concha,
Who stood in the door not daring to enter.

                              The girl
Appeared kneeling, only her knees were lifted
A little above the floor; her head devoutly
Drooped over. She was naked but the bandaged arm;
The coins about the small nipples were now
As black as Concha's; the lips dark, the fine skin
Mottled with lead-color. Ilaria pushed in and lifted
The body, Jesus Acanna then found his knife
And cut the strap. They stretched the slender body
On the bed and began to talk, but Dante Vitello
Remembered at length to pump the ribs with his hands.
They saw the lids of the eyes after a time
Flutter and close; the Swiss paused from his labor,
The breathing went on by itself.

                              Cawdor returned
From the Rock with Michal, but would not enter the house.
He seemed going toward the sea when she left him. He went
As far as the work-shop and fetched tools for digging,
A lantern, matches to light it. He chose the tools
With a clear mind; this work had to be done
Because of the coyotes. It proved more dreadful
Than he'd imagined; but when it was done the dreadfulness
    itself
Had purged his mind of emotion. He took no pains
To conceal the grave, for at this time discovery
Meant nothing to him, he desired nor feared nothing,
Not even to put back time and undo an act.
However, no person ever went up there.
He rolled stones on the grave against the coyotes,

And gathered the tools, but when he had carried them
Half way home, he threw them with the lantern too
Into the creek under the starless redwoods.
His mind ceased there, as if the tools had been strings
Between the world and his mind; these cut, it closed.

In the bright of dawn, before sunrise began,
The lank steers wheeled their line when he waved his arms.
He cursed them with obscene words . . . but why? . . . and there
    stood
Thirty in a row, all in a row like soldiers
Staring at him with strained-up heads. He was in the pasture
On the highest dome of the hill.
Wild fragrant wind blew from the burning east,
A handful of cloud high up in the air caught fire and vanished.
A point of more excessive light appeared
On the ridge by the lone oak and enlarged.
Without doubt, the sun. But if it were the horn of a flaming
    beast:
We'd have a horned beast to see by.
"What have I lost by doing through a blind accident
What I ought to have done in cold blood? Was Hood anything
    to me?
I have lost nothing." He'd have counted Fera
Lost, if he'd thought of Fera; she did not enter his mind.
"If I'd lost much: it's likely I'd not lie down
But gather again and go on." His flesh and bones were soaked
With aching weariness: but that was nothing either.
His eyes dazzled in the rivers of light
And the sea lay at his feet flat and lifeless
Far down, but flecked with the steps of the wind. He went down
    to the house
And heard that Fera had hanged herself and been saved,
But that was nothing either. No, something. "Where were you?"
He said to Concha. "She send me down. She send me.

She send me down for water. When I come back: Oh!"
"I'll not see her this morning," he answered.
"Bring my clothes to the little room on the north,
And change the bed there. Hood's gone for good." He had done
    justly,
And could sleep very well there.

                            Two days passed
Before he remembered the blanket-roll and the rifle
Dropped in the oaks when Michal came. He went and sought
But never found them. But that was nothing either.

XII

Her voice was still roughened with an off whisper
In the bruised throat, and the white of one of her eyes
Grained with a drop of red, a little blood-vessel
Had broken there when the strap drew. When she was alone
She lay pointed on the bed, stiffened to the attitude
Of formal death, feeling the ache in her arm
But hardly conscious of it, the hours and scenes
And the form as a whole of all her life incessantly
Moving behind the blank wide open eyes.
She lay and contemplated it with little emotion
And hardly a thought. She thought of herself as dead.
Although she knew perfectly that she was living,
And had said to Concha: "You needn't watch me, you and Ilaria.
I'll never try death again, now I understand
That to fail is the very soul of my soul.
Failure is not so sweet that one who feels it
Beforehand will go running to meet it again.
Though death is sweet. That will come in its time,

When I'm as old as my father, I fear not sooner;
Never for the asking."

                              She said to Concha another day:
"I wish you could get Michal to come and see me;
Or George even. Not one soul has come in,
Not since the doctor was here, and death is so lonesome.
I could get up, but when I begin to walk
Cawdor will send me away. You must never tell them
That I can get up." This was at noon; Concha
Painfully made a slow thought in her mind
All afternoon, and said to Cawdor in the evening,
Stammering, because her words were planned beforehand:
"She say that she is well enough to get up."
"Who says?" "Oh . . . she . . .." "You mean," he said frowning,
"My wife? Let her get up then." She turned sadly, and then said:
"When she get up you going to send her away?"
"What is that to you?" Then Concha recklessly: "You keep her
After she loving with Hood?" She curved her body
In fear of his hand; but he took hold of her wrist
And drove her up the stairway to Fera's room.

Who lay in the bed straightened to the shape of death
And looked at them with still eyes; the scarlet drop
In the white of the left one spoiled her eyes' peace. Cawdor
Put off the questions that had burned him to ask,
And stood still and then said: "You are well enough to get up,
Concha says, but you think I'd send you away."
She smiled at Concha. "I wondered whether you'd do it.
And then I thought you wouldn't, but it's no matter.
No: you won't send me," she said to Cawdor, "for I
Suffered my destruction in simple innocence.
Oh, certainly you'll not drink again from a mouthed cup,

But the cup's not blamed. You are much too just to punish
  the cup. There are more reasons." His face a moment
Was like her father's a scar; it formed itself to be dark metal
  again and he said: "No doubt
You were loving with him and so he went mad." She thought,
  and answered: "No. You did justice. I know what you did.
You'd better send out your brown tattle-tales
Before we say any more, she'd hear and go tell, wouldn't
  you Concha? Besides that her sour odor
Poisons the room. I've noticed lately, the living smell much
  worse than the dead. Oh, never mourn them;
No one was ever sorry to have died." He shook his head, like
  the bull that has charged a man and found
Only the vacant flapping of a red blanket, and he said:
  "Be straight will you for once, I won't hurt you.
You hide in a smoke of words like lies. Perhaps"—his face
  hollowed with terror—"it was all a lie?
No, that can't be. You white poison, you were in the boat with
  him and lied
To save your skin?" He turned on Concha: "Did you see her make
  love to him?" But the Indian woman feared to go on;
She shook her head, and looked aside at Fera, and shook her
  head. Cawdor made himself patient
And said, "Perhaps a kiss: or you saw her stroking his head:
  he had fine hair . . . ." Fera lay faintly
Smiling and watched him; he looked, stooping his face to Concha's,
  like a tall old Jew bargaining, and said:
"Or you saw them . . . by God, you told me they kissed, you said
  that." She nodded her head, panting and shrinking backward,
Wiping her dark hands on her apron incessantly; and Fera: "She'll
  tell more lies if you make more faces,
And when that fails you could pinch her arm. How can you expect
  truth from such people, they're all afraid of you?"
He looked at Concha and said feebly: "If I could know.

I am stupid and things are hidden. What I have done.
    Was right, but the blood rushes me behind my eyes
And God sends chance. It all happened in the blindness of chance."
    Fera said quietly "Don't talk before her."
He looked at her eyes and said, "You have the secret, if I could
    trust you. That red drop comes from hanging
And will clear up. You seem quieter in mind
Than ever before. Do you know where I sleep now? Hood's room."
    "It was Concha's first." He groaned in his throat, feeling
That every thought in her mind was impure, how could he fish
    the truth from a dirty fountain? He said:
"And yet you'll tell me. It will make no difference to you but only
    to me. I will do nothing to punish you,
Whatever you say, nothing in your favor either." "I've told you
    already," she answered. "But whether you tempted him,
Invited him, you egged him on, you thought he was safe. A word:
    or only a damned smile: women
Can move hell with their eyes." She closed her eyes, and said,
    keeping them closed: "What I said that night
Each word was true. You're right though, I've still a secret. Shoo
    tattle-tales out,
And then I'll tell you my secret." He said, "Concha:
    get out." She sighed and went out gladly, and Fera:
"Open the door; I won't have her at the door." However
    the hallway was empty, and Fera said:
"I was friendly with him, he was your son and Michal's brother.
    I never in act nor look nor thought
Stepped over that. Was he vicious when he was little? I never
    knew it. A beast lived in his blood,
But no one warned me and now he is gone." "That's the word:
    gone. You are safe to blacken him, he can't answer."
"If I should lie and whiten him," she said,
"And say he was innocent, some stitch of his nerves in him
    destroyed me but his heart was innocent: and you believed it:

How could you sleep? And after a night or two
That room you have taken might seem too little for you.
    You are very strong, you'd hold yourself quiet three night,
Or four nights, and then wander on the hill scaring the cattle."
    He said gravely, "Does every one know?
Who told you this?" "No one," she answered. "And after a week
    of nights they'd find you with those big-boned
Fingers clenched in your throat quiet on the hill." "On the Rock,"
    he said. "Oh, on the Rock. But since . . .
Or under the Rock. But since he was guilty you can sleep sound."
    The flesh of his face, that had sagged lately,
Was now become firm for danger, and he asked: "How do you
    know these things if no one watched me?" She answered,
"I know you so well. I used to be near you, if you remember,
    before I was spoiled. And now, lying
Like this"—she lay pointed in the bed, her arms on her breast—
    "I mean alone and cut off from life,
I've had leisure and power to think of you plainly, so all your
    acts that night stand in my mind
Fixed and forever like pieces of stone. That's the way with
    us dead, we see things whole and never
Wonder at things." He said, "You lie here and dream and imagine.
    There's nothing in it." "So you won't send me,"
She answered, "to stay with strangers. I know too much and might
    tell: that's nothing to you: but as time darkens
You'll find me the only comforter you have. And I can teach
    you the way to blessedness: I've tasted life
And tasted death; the one's warm water, yellow with
    mud and wrigglers, sucked from a puddle in the road,
Or hot water that scalds you to screaming;
The other is bright and cool and quiet, drawn from the deep.
    You knocked the scummed cup from the boy's hand
And gave him the other: is that a thing to be sorry for? I know;
    I have both in my hands; life's on the broken

And splinted left, so I never lift it. You did kindly, not terribly.
   If you were wise, you'd do
As much for yourself. If you were loving you'd do
As much for me." He stood and listened, and said "Is that all?"
She nodded. "Then it's not much.
I see there are two of us here twisting in hell,
Smile as you like." "Why yes," she answered, "by the left arm.
That's true. But I taste both." He was leaving the room
And she cried after him: "Oh my dear, dear, be merciful.
Life is so tough to cut, I never would have dreamed.
I fail. But nothing stops *you*."

                  He went out-doors
And felt a seeming-irresistible desire
To go to the foot of the Rock and lie with those stones
On the soft earth, his mouth whispering against it.
But now, he must never give in to any desire;
Strain the iron forever. Never do anything strange:
For even now their eyes followed him strangely.
No matter; they'd keep in subjection; they might have watched it
And not dare speak: but a pity if little Michal . . . .
The stars in the sparse boughs, the skies are never
Darkened any more, a naughty glitter.
How does one commonly spend a winter evening:
Not letting the stars glitter through the split boughs.
He entered the house and sat down. Strain the iron forever:
He had strength for that.

                Fera had little strength,
And the long hollow night coming looked unendurable.
Her right arm was flung free of the cover and lay
Bent on her eyes; after a while her teeth
Found the wrist: ugh, what was this? She raised it and saw
The yellow and brown scabs of the laceration
Where she had gnawed it before.

82

In the morning, when Concha
Came in to serve her, she said "Did you believe in heaven and hell
When you were little? (To-day I'll get up,
I've had enough of this bed, you'll help me dress.)
Because you know the dead rarely come back;
But I died and came back, and I can tell you
More than the priests know. Dying's not bad: Oh, bad enough,
But you can stand it, you have to. But afterwards . . . Ah, there's . . .."
She moaned, her tight small fist crept up to her cheek
And trembled there. She was playing a comedy, she played
          it so well
Her own flesh suffered and chilled. "Death is no sleep, Concha,
          death is eternal torment and terror
For all that die. Neither is there any heaven for anyone.
          I saw my father there crying blood
From the hollows of his blind eyes and tearing his beard with
          his hands. He said 'Oh my God have you come, Fera?
Who ever dreamed that death could be worse than life?' I said
          'It is so,' and all the crowd of the dead
Began moaning 'It is so.' But then you managed to make
          me breathe with your hands and I could come back,
They said to me then, 'Never tell any living person what death
          is like, for if they imagined
What it's like, for they all must come, how could they live?
Who'd not go mad with fear to feel it approaching?'
Oh Concha, hug life with tooth and nail, for what
Comes after is the most horrible. And no end, no end.
(Come here and help me. We'll have to slit down the sleeve
And pin it over the shoulder.) I didn't tell you
To scare you, Concha. Don't think about it. Ah no,
Or we'd sit screaming.
I wasn't going to tell you but then I thought
That you can bear it as well as I can, after the trick
You played me last night, my rival!
Live. Live forever if you could. Oh it was frightful."

XIII

Though she was up, and began to live and go out,
She avoided Cawdor's presence, still fearing to be sent away
If seen too often. She kept her room at meal-times,
And he was almost never about the house
The other hours of the day.

                              The first time she went out,
She only walked under the storm-broken cypresses
About the door and went in; but the next morning
She climbed the steep to the great oak by the graves.
Still weak and bloodless, dizzy with climbing, she lay
Face down on the dug earth, her mouth breathing against it
And whispering over her father's body below.
The grave retained its freshness, no rain had fallen
On the red earth. She heard after a time
A rustling and scraping noise and raised her head.
It was Michal's eagle hungrily astir in the cage;
She used to feed it about this time. Fera
Saw beak and eyes in the shadow, and the dark square
Of the box cage against the bright blue shining
Flat ocean and the arch of sky. She stood up, and walked
About the oak's bole; she seemed to be counting the graves,
But there were only three; the two ancient ones
Enclosed with pickets and the raw new one unfenced.

Michal came up with flesh and water for the eagle,
But Fera stood on the other side of the oak
Until she had come; then, coming forward from it:
"Why Michal, how strange to think that all these days,
No matter what's happened, you still go on steadily as sunrise.
My father dies of old age, I fish for death

And catch failure again, and Hood . . . but you and the sunrises
Go on as if our tears and our deaths were nothing.
He isn't glad to see you: I'd have been glad to see you,
My lonely days in bed, but you never came."
Michal had looked over her shoulder, her face
Growing white as it turned. She turned back to the cage.
"I didn't know you were here," she said, and poured out
The dirty water from the drinking-basin
Without turning again. "I see that you hate me,"
Fera said; "we'll not speak of that. I see that your father
Has thought *my* father's grave not worthy of a mark.
If the cold charity of the county had buried him
There'd be a stake with his name.
Yet he was here like a man among cattle,
The only mind in this ditch." Michal said nothing,
But rubbed the white slime from the basin and rinsed it,
And Fera said, "The oak's dying, they chopped its roots.
Or was it the storm that burned these baby leaves?
We ought to be friends, Michal." Michal set in
The filled basin and shut the door of the cage.
She opened her lips to speak, and then kept silence,
And Fera said, "You'll listen, my dear, if you won't speak.
    Do you think I'll swallow
These white and hating looks as if they were earned?
    What have I done? Tried to die? Yes; I tried twice;
And that was stupid, but people are pitied for that, not hated.
    You were quite kind my days of sunshine,
And now you peck the feathers from the sick bird." Michal said
    trembling, "Oh, no. Not that I'm spiteful,
Only, I can't understand." "That's true," she answered,
    "how could you?
Your life has been sweet and full of ignorance. But I, when
    my father was drunk in town, would hear my mother
Take lovers in the house. *There* was somebody to hate. Yet they
    were white men;

They weren't the color of Concha . . . no more of that. The second
    time I died I almost made it, you know.
They pumped me alive with their hands and I was born again
From the dark air: since then I can understand much that
    was dark before. So you, Michal,
Will understand . . . many things that are dark . . . when some
    wild night kills childhood in you. That's coming:
But don't pray for it, my dear.
Oh, Michal that's the reason I so much want you to listen
    to me. The inflamed and dark season
And bitterness will come, and then I dread your saying
    to yourself: 'Fera she hated life; Fera
Preferred death; Fera was wise.' I wasn't; at least you mustn't
    think so. I welched on my fate,
(And failed of course, failure's my root in nature) but I am ashamed.
    So you must listen to me, Michal,
My praise of life, by my dead father, by the dying oak. What
    I've lived has not been lucky you know,
If I can praise it, who'd not? But how good it is, Michal, to live!
    Good for what? Ah, there's the question.
For the pleasure of it? Hardly for that. Take your own life, mine's
    marked, mine's worse than usual. Your mother
Lies yonder; you never knew her, you missed the *pleasure*
    of knowing her. You missed the pains too; you might
    have hated her.
More likely you'd have loved her deeply; you'd have been
    sad then to see her wasting with age and pain,
Those years would come; and you'd have felt the salt fountains
    of loneliness
Drain from your eyes when the day came and she died. There's
    not a pleasure in the world not paid for, Michal,
In pain with a penny or two for interest. But youth, they
    say, is a shining time, and no doubt for you
The pleasures outsun the pains. Then the hair grays, and the teeth
    blacken or drop, and the sky blackens.

You've swollen ankles and shrunk thighs, and horrible hanging
    breasts that flap like a hound's ears,
Or death comes first . . . .. Oh, but I'm wrong, it's life I was praising!
    And the pain to the pleasure is sun to candle.
Joy never kills, you know, the most violent joy
Never drove anyone mad. Pain kills, and pain drives
    mad; and extreme pain can feed for days
On the stretched flesh; the extremes of pleasure rot in two
    minutes.

              Oh yes, but, Michal,
Surely life's . . . good? My father—his thoughts were deep,
Patient and wise—believed it was good because it was growing.
At first it was a morsel of slime on the sea,
It grew to be worms and fishes, lizards and snakes,
You see the progress, then things with hair and hot blood,
It was coming up from the ocean and climbing mountains,
Subduing the earth, molding its bundle of nerves
Into the magnificent mind of man, and passing
Beyond man, to more wonders. That helped my father!
He loved that. You and me of course it can't help,
Because we know nothing goes on forever.
What good is better and better if best draws blank?
Here's the oak was growing upward a hundred years
And now it withers. Sometime the world
Will change, only a little too hot or too cold
Or too dry, and then life will go like the oak.
Then what will all my father's magnificent thought,
Michal, and all the dreams of your children be worth?
Well, we must praise life for some other reason.
For surely it's . . . good? We know it must be. Here every morning
You bring food to this bird to keep it alive:
Because you love it: in its filth, in misery, in prison. What's
    wretcheder than a caged eagle? Guess. I'll not tell.

And you'd be bitter cruel to keep it alive: sick-feathered, abject,
    broken-armed: only, you know,
Life is so *good.* It's true the creature seems ungrateful:
    but I am not grateful either; to Dante
Vitello who pumped the breath into my body."
She stopped and looked at Michal's white face, and said
"You haven't heard from Hood yet? He went so suddenly,
He ought to write you." Michal said "No," and Fera:
"You know nothing about him?" She cried trembling:
"Why do you ask about Hood? Why do you ask about Hood?
Let me alone." "Ah," Fera said, "do you think
That something has happened to him?" "He'll never come back.
It was your fault." "I'm sure he'll never come back,"
She said with a still face. "Now let's go down.
But I can't joke about your eagle, Michal.
The hopeless cage of pain is a lamp
Shining rays that go right through the flesh
And etch the secrets of bone. Mine aches. Oh no, Michal,
I couldn't do it: but George would kill him for you:
Or ask your father: that's better: those are the hands."

Another morning Fera went up
Secretly under the redwoods to the Rock's foot,
Where the great ribbed and battering granite face
Came down and found earth. In spring the cliff-swallows nest
A third of the way up, and a pair of duck-hawks
Two thirds of the way. High in the air the gray dome
Seemed swaying from the sweep of the small fibrous clouds.
Fera crept back and forth at the foot with pale
Spying eyes: but this loose earth was only a squirrel's mound,
And that was a gopher's digging: for hours: and she found
Stones had been rolled together, their brown earth-bellies
Turned up to the sky, and the gray lichenous backs
Downward, there was fresh earth below, with grass-blades
Half buried, and ferns trampled. One rain had fallen.

She stood and gazed and said to him there:
  "Did I not say beforehand
That after we were dead I should have no rest after
  all but run moaning
On the gray shore, gnawing for my hunger a wrist of shadow?"
  She found a brown scurf on the slope rocks
Above, and thought, "This is the blood that burst from your
  mouth when you fell"; caressing with hers the doubtful
Crust, that was really a brown lichen. "Oh, why would
  you not listen to me? You chose to die
Rather than live. Ah, you'd learned wisdom somewhere, you were
  too young to be wise, when with one beautiful
Act of delight, lovely to the giver as the taker, you might have
  made
A star for yourself and for me salvation." She rose and said
  to the grave: "It was I that killed you. The old man
Who lives in hell for it was only my hands."

XIV

It was true; and it was Cawdor that paid the suffering.
The woman found ease in words and outcry; the man,
The more sensitive by sex and by his nature,
Had forbidden himself action because one act
Was grown his cancer; speech because speech betrays;
Even thought, in one regard, for if Hood's guilt
Were not monstrous and the punishment became monstrous,
And if he had been solicited into adultery
His guilt was not monstrous but halved and natural;
There was evidence enough for that, and there
Thought was forbidden. Meanwhile his mind remained
Implacably clear for the rest, cloudless harsh light
On what he had done, memory not dimmed with time

But magnified and more real, not masked with any
Mysticism, that comes most often and stands
Between the criminal and his crime, a redeemer
Shifting the load onto fate; no failure toward unreason
Except the fantasy of his wife's innocence.

His loved canyon was grown hateful and terrible;
He longed to go away, go away, but that
Was cowardice, the set pride and code of his life
Prohibited that; he desired to kill himself,
But that was cowardice; to go and accuse himself,
But that was a kind of cowardice; all the outlets of action
Were locked and locked. But the most present desire,
And the most self-despised, was to ask advice
No matter of whom: of George, of Dante Vitello:
He yearned on them with his eyes: but that was cowardice
And ridiculous too. Day by day the tensions of his mind
Were screwed tighter in silence. He had some strength,
Though not the strength his vanity used to imagine,
And now in the deadlock of his powers endurance
Continued still. He felt the eyes of his house
That used to peer at him from behind now openly
Glitter before his face. He believed they all knew,
Save little Michal, and were kept quiet by fear,
They watched his face for weakness, as the blackbirds
In Carmel Valley watch the green fruit for softness.

After the flood in December the later rains
Fell scant, shrewd north wind heeling listless falls
Blew the hills dry; Cawdor discovered his mind
Building conjectural bridges between the drought
And the curse of his deed; he conquered the sick thought,
Another cowardice.

In March when the cows were calving
Came printed news of foot-and-mouth disease
Among the cattle in the North, it had come in
Through San Francisco from Asia. An infected herd
Had been destroyed. Cawdor read and feared nothing,
His herd in the isolation of the coast canyon
Would be the last. Yet he dreamed in the night
That he was slaughtering his herd. A bench was dug
To stand on, in the steep wall of a gully;
He stood there with the sledge-hammer and Jesus Acanna
All black on a black horse against the twilight
Drove in the cattle. One swing of the hammer for each
On the peak between the horns, but the white-faced heifer
Sidled her head and the blow crushed the horn.
Bawling and slopped with blood down the sleek shoulders,
Plunging among the carcasses . . .. The dream returned
Too many times; the plague increasing in the north
He warned his men to guard the pasture and watch
For strays; then the dream ceased; but the hurt heifer
Still troubled his dreams.

                His mind had relented toward Fera,
Innocent sufferer and as wretched as himself.
He saw now that both George and Michal hated her.
Her arm had knitted crooked, it pained always
In her pale eyes. He spoke to her kindly; she answered patiently.
He saw as in a vision that if he should choose
He might go back to his own room from Hood's
This very night, and all be as it was before.
To hell with the glittering eyes, they would keep quiet.
"No," he said and went out of the house. But she
Followed and overtook him under the cypresses
In the evening twilight.

                    Michal and George were left
In the lamplight in the room, and Michal said
"I want you . . ." she made more words but they were
    too mumbled
To understand; she stopped and drew breath and said
Astonishingly aloud, as if she were calling
Across a canyon: "I want you to kill my eagle.
I ought never to have kept it. Nothing but wretchedness.
George, will you kill it quickly and without pain
To-morrow morning?" He stared at her and said
"We've other troubles to think of." "Yes. If you won't
I'll do it myself." "I will. Don't cry, Michal."
She went up-stairs crying.

                        In the twilight under the trees
Fera touched Cawdor's arm and said timidly: "The best
Would be not to've been born at all; but if we are bound to live
    why should we hate each other?"
He turned in surprise, he had forgotten her. "You are not bound."
    "By failures of nature. I am like a sick beast . . .
Like Michal's eagle . . . I can't do for myself. I've tried. Think
    of me a little. You did the other
No evil but eternal good. Forget him now, and if I can't
    end: failure's my peg that I hang on:
Mayn't we go back and live as we were before? You loved
    me once, when I was a child and you
Were a man." He stood silent thinking of another matter,
    suddenly he barked with laughter and said,
"What am I now?" "A living God: you could answer prayer
    if you pleased." "Don't be troubled," he said,
"About God. You talk about God
The day before you go mad." "I can't do that either. Are you afraid
    to live," she answered,
"Because they whisper? But they know nothing; they've
    not a thread of evidence. I've talked to them all, not one

    92

But I, not one but I could betray you." She peered up at his face
    to see what it said in the twilight.
It said nothing; he was thinking of another matter, and walking
    the open way from the trees, slowly
Toward the sea's fading light. "Besides, they are all afraid
of you. Oh listen!" she said. "We two alone
Have all the decision. Nobody but I can twitch the reins in your
    hands. Look at me." She caught his arm.
"Am I changed?" He looked, and suddenly laughed with pleasure.
    "Why . . . like a blown-out candle. Perfectly changed.
The fragrance all gone, all the wind fallen." He failed
    to see the lightning pallor, he was so prisoned
In the surprise of his mind. "No more in my eyes than a dead
    stick. No more," he said in astonishment,
"Than Concha Rosas." He spoke with no intention of cruelty,
    his mind in the pain of its own bonds
Islanded alone, incapable of feeling another's. She clasped
    her throat with her hand and said shuddering:
"For this. No, not another time.
I went on my knees to Hood, I made myself a shameless beggar,
    I washed his feet with tears.
That's not done twice. To love me: and he would not
Ah, God how can I make you know it? I duped you too well.
    Ah, dupe, Ah, fool," she stammered, "Ah, murderer.
Machine that one winds up and it goes and does it. I wound
    you, I was the one. Now the air's fire
To drink and the days and nights the teeth and throat
    of a dog: shall I hide your eyes with my hand always
From what you have done, to let you die in sweet ignorance?"
    He said, "Go on. Strain it out, gasping, a heifer
With the first calf." "It's the only child I'll bear you. I hope
    you will like the child. You killed the other
Woman's but mine perhaps will spill *you*
From the same rock. For proofs: ask Michal, she heard me pray
    to him for love: ask Concha Rosas again,

The fat beast listened and saw, she heard me, she helped me fool
      you: ask Jesus Acanna,
Watched me lead Hood from my father's earth to the laurel
      to be my lover: *I* led him, *I* called him, *I* flung
Flowers and fire at his feet: he never at mine: and he refused
      me, he died for that. Ask your eyes,
Heartless blue stones in their caves, wanted to be blind and they
      saw,
They saw me come down in the rain to call him, the rain steamed
      where it struck, I was hot, I walked in a shameless
Burning heat; my father was dying but I ran down.
And again you saw me, Hood was naked in bed at dawn,
      you caught me in his room. Had he received me
Gladly or kindly, had he raised his arms to receive me? I begged
      and he put me by, I broke in to beg
And he was driving me out when you came. He remembered
      his father's honor, he was a fool and faithful,
He's paid for it, he was faithful to you, you paid the wages.
      Ah, wait, I've more.
It's precious to me to tell you these things, I've hardly desired
      honey-sweet death a longer while."
"You lie too much," he answered, "I asked you before to tell
      me. Pour it out."
He stood like a gray tree in the twilight, only a surface trembling,
      the axe was blunted in the bark,
Fera thought; and she said: "I asked him to cut leaves from
      the laurel to lay in my father's grave,
There are no flowers in this ditch,
And under the laurel I gave him my love. Are you glad that
      he had my love? That saves you, that lets you live.
The old husband happy in his wife's pleasures.
Under the laurel it was, behind the concealing oaks, under
      the laurel it was. Before,
I had only cried out and begged with tears, but there I gave
      him my body, my arms about him, my breasts

94

Against him: be patient will you, this is not much, this is not the
poison: I gave him my flesh to eat,
As Michal takes up meat to the eagle, but he was wilder than
the eagle.
He remembered his father's honor, he would not feed. My arms
were his cage, I held the meat to his mouth,
He would not feed." Her face distorted itself and seemed to reflect
flame, like the white smoke
Of a hidden fire of green wood shining at night, twisting as it rises.
Gipsies crouch by the smoke's root
Watching strange flesh simmer in the pot between the forked
sticks. When the wind varies their eyes prickle
And the shine of the smoke hides the gray stars. Her face writhed
like the shining smoke and she cried and said:
"I wish the little rivers under the laughing kingfishers in every
canyon were fire, and the ocean
Fire, and my heart not afraid to go down.
I broke my heart against his mouth like honeycomb, he would
not take me, Oh, the bitter honey, the black-blooded
Drops from the wax, no wonder he refused me. There
was a lion-skin
I wore to my death, was it you stole it or Concha? He gave
it to me, his one gift, but your house
Is a house of thieves. One boy was honest and so you killed
him. The boy respected his father's possession.
He despised me, he spat me out. Then when I pressed him hard
and set fire to his body: the heart and soul
I never could reach, they were both stones: he took his hunter's
knife in his hand, he made the pain
Of the point in his flesh a servant against me. Into his thigh
he drove it, he laughed and was lame, and triumphed,
And limped into the darkness of death."

                              She stood silent, and
        Cawdor remembered his son's lameness

Stumbling under the old man's coffin up the steep hill.
He groaned aloud, then Fera's face
Gleaming spotted the darkness before his eyes. "I loved him,"
she said. "Love is a trap that takes
The trapper and his game in the same teeth. The first
to die has the luck. They hang bleeding together.
But you were a mere dupe and a common murderer,
Not love but envy, dupe and fool, what will you do?"
He swayed against the dark hill, "You make the lies,"
He said hoarsely, "must I always believe them?
Time. Time. All my damnation draws
From having done in a haste. What do you want?"
"If I were you
And had your strength I'd kill the woman first,
Then cut out the eyes that couldn't tell my innocent
Boy's head from a calf's to butcher,
And smell my way to the Rock and take the jump."
"I asked you," he said, "because a known devil's
Word is a warning." She came and touched him. "The first's
Easiest," she said, "to kill the woman: the rest
Follows of its own accord." She stroked his face and said
"It is all easy." He took her throat in his hands,
She did not tremble nor flinch; he tightened his fingers
Slowly, as if he were dreaming the thing, not doing it,
Then her mouth opened, but the ivory face
Kept its composure still; his fingers closed
A little harder and half checked the hot breath.
Suddenly she clawed at his hands with hers, she cried
"Have pity! I didn't mean it. Oh, Oh, I was lying.
Let me live!" He set her by and ran back to the house,
She heard him sob as he ran.

                    George was alone
In the lamp-lit room, Cawdor came in and said
"It's nothing," and went up-stairs, his eyes so sunken

That no gleam showed. He shut himself in the room
He used now, where Hood had slept before. George followed
Quietly and saw the crack under the door
Silent of light; he listened and heard no sound.
Then he returned down-stairs. Fera had come in;
She made a smile and passed him and went to her place.

XV

In the morning Cawdor failed to come down; Michal
At length knocked at his door. She listened, trembling,
And got no answer. She opened the door. He stood
Against the window and said "Is it you Michal?
I'm not well. Let me alone." She saw that the bed
Had not been slept in; she could not see his face
Against the shining light, but his voice frightened her,
So gentle and forlorn. "Let me bring you some breakfast,
Father?" "No," he said, "no. But there's one thing
You could do for me." "What thing?" "To let me alone.
Nothing else. Nothing else." She saw that his face
Kept turning toward the bed, the eyes and features
Could hardly be seen against the morning light.
She thought he meant to lie down.

                              When Michal had gone
He locked the door, and leaning to the bed whispered:
"She didn't see you. How astonished she'd have been,
She thinks you're hunting in the north." He smiled fondly
And touched the pillow. "You always had fine hair
But now it has grown longer." A sad perplexity
Wrinkled his face; when he drew back his hand
His eyes were again serene. He went to the window

And stood with his back against the light. "From here
I see you the most clearly. Ah, no, lie quiet.
You've had a fall," he said shaking, "don't speak.
This puts my eyes in heaven." He stood a long while
And his face darkened. "She keeps begging to die.
Plenty of others want that and make less noise.
It was only a sorrowful joke last night,
I'd not have done it. I made her beg off at least.
But when she squealed I hardly could let go,
My fingers cramped like the arms of breeding toads.
I've lived some months in pain."

                       He listened, and said:
"I know. Thank God. But if you had died, what then?
I had too much foolish pride to throw the game
Because it hurt." He paused and said "I thought
I needed punishment but death's no punishment.
I thought of telling the sheriff": he laughed. "I know him.
And a judge save me? I had to judge myself.
Run to a judge was only running away
From judgment; I thought I'd not do that; shame Michal
And do no good. Running away. I thought the same
Of killing myself. Oh, I've been thinking.
If I'd believed in hellfire I'd have done it
Most nights of the week." He listened, and shook his head.
"No value in needless pain? Oh, yet if I lay
As damned with blood as I believed I was
I'd manage somehow. Tit for tat is good sense.
The debt was to myself as well as to you,
And mostly I've paid my debts. Well, I thank God.
This black's turned gray."

                    Michal had found her brother
Mending iron at the forge, the little shed
Behind the work-shop; she'd heard the hammer and found him.

"Have you forgotten your promise?" "Why, no," George
    answered,
"I'll do it for you. I thought you'd change your mind."
She was as pale as if a dear friend's death
Were being sealed in the plot. "Then do it quickly.
I think that father," she said, "is going to be sick.
Our lives perhaps will change, I'll not have time
For trapping squirrels to notch the dreary days
Of the cage with pitiful instants of pleasure." He frowned
And struck the iron, the red darkening, with scales
Of black, and white flecks.

                              While George went to the house
For his revolver, Michal climbed up the hill
Weeping; but when he came with death in his hand
She'd not go away, but watched. At the one shot
The great dark bird leaped at the roof of the cage
In silence and struck the wood; it fell, then suddenly
Looked small and soft, muffled in its folded wings.

The nerves of men after they die dream dimly
And dwindle into their peace; they are not very passionate,
And what they had was mostly spent while they lived.
They are sieves for leaking desire; they have many pleasures
And conversations; their dreams too are like that.
The unsocial birds are a greater race;
Cold-eyed, and their blood burns. What leaped up to death,
The extension of one storm-dark wing filling its world,
Was more than the soft garment that fell. Something had flown
    away. Oh cage-hoarded desire,
Like the blade of a breaking wave reaped by the wind, or flame
    rising from fire, or cloud-coiled lightning
Suddenly unfurled in the cave of heaven: I that am stationed,
    and cold at heart, incapable of burning,

My blood like standing sea-water lapped in a stone pool,
    my desire to the rock, how can I speak of you?
Mine will go down to the deep rock.

                                    This rose,
Possessing the air over its emptied prison,
The eager powers at its shoulders waving shadowless
Unwound the ever-widened spirals of flight
As a star light, it spins the night-stabbing threads
From its own strength and substance: so the aquiline desire
Burned itself into meteor freedom and spired
Higher still, and saw the mountain-dividing
Canyon of its captivity (that was to Cawdor
Almost his world) like an old crack in a wall,
Violet-shadowed and gold-lighted; the little stain
Spilt on the floor of the crack was the strong forest;
The grain of sand was the Rock. A speck, an atomic
Center of power clouded in its own smoke
Ran and cried in the crack; it was Cawdor; the other
Points of humanity had neither weight nor shining
To prick the eyes of even an eagle's passion.

This burned and soared. The shining ocean below lay on the shore
Like the great shield of the moon come down, rolling bright
    rim to rim with the earth. Against it the multiform
And many-canyoned coast-range hills were gathered into
    one carven mountain, one modulated
Eagle's cry made stone, stopping the strength of the sea. The
    beaked and winged effluence
Felt the air foam under its throat and saw
The mountain sun-cup Tassajara, where fawns
Dance in the stream of the hot fountains at dawn,
Smoothed out, and the high strained ridges beyond Cachagua,
Where the rivers are born and the last condor is dead,
Flatten, and a hundred miles toward morning the Sierras

Dawn with their peaks of snow, and dwindle and smooth down
On the globed earth.

        It saw from the height and desert space
   of unbreathable air
Where meteors make green fire and die, the ocean dropping
   westward to the girdle of the pearls of dawn
And the hinder edge of the night sliding toward Asia;
   it saw far under eastward the April-delighted
Continent; and time relaxing about it now, abstracted from being,
   it saw the eagles destroyed,
Mean generations of gulls and crows taking their world: turn
   for turn in the air, as on earth
The white faces drove out the brown. It was the white decayed
   and the brown from Asia returning;
It saw men learn to outfly the hawk's brood and forget it again;
   it saw men cover the earth and again
Devour each other and hide in caverns, be scarce as wolves.
   It neither wondered nor cared, and it saw
Growth and decay alternate forever, and the tides returning.

It saw, according to the sight of its kind, the archetype
Body of life a beaked carnivorous desire
Self-upheld on storm-broad wings: but the eyes
Were spouts of blood; the eyes were gashed out; dark blood
Ran from the ruinous eye-pits to the hook of the beak
And rained on the waste spaces of empty heaven.
Yet the great Life continued; yet the great Life.
Was beautiful, and she drank her defeat, and devoured
Her famine for food.

      There the eagle's phantom perceived
Its prison and its wound were not its peculiar wretchedness,
All that lives was maimed and bleeding, caged or in blindness,
Lopped at the ends with death and conception, and shrewd

Cautery of pain on the stumps to stifle the blood, but not
Refrains for all that; life was more than its functions
And accidents, more important than its pains and pleasures,
A torch to burn in with pride, a necessary
Ecstasy in the run of the cold substance,
And scape-goat of the greater world. (But as for me,
I have heard the summer dust crying to be born
As much as ever flesh cried to be quiet.)
Pouring itself on fulfilment the eagle's passion
Left life behind and flew at the sun, its father.
The great unreal talons took peace for prey
Exultantly, their death beyond death; stooped upward,
    and struck
Peace like a white fawn in a dell of fire.

XVI

Cawdor in the room in the house, his eyes fixed
On the empty bed: "Age tells. I've known the time . . .
But now from having fasted a night of sleep
After some bad ones, my eyes have a dazzle in them
So that I sometimes lose your face, then instantly
The trouble returns. I was cut deep:
But never half my deserving." He heard a listener
Lean at the door and the latch move a little;
His face blanked and was still. After long silence
A gentle tapping, and spoken through the shut door:
"I think you are not well: let me in a moment.
Your voice has been going on and on like fever
And now why has it stopped?" Cawdor stood shaking
Like a gray horse tethered short to the fence,
Unable to rear or step back, a serpent rattling
Its passionate sistrum in the lupin by the hooves.

He extended hands toward the bed, his eyes widened
To hold their vision, but as he feared it vanished,
Then he was not able to restrain his hands
From feeling the length of the bed, patting and stroking
Where there was nothing but the smooth coverlet.
He stood and hardened himself, the knocking renewed.
"I have been deceived. It began in the dark,"
He whispered, "and I've dreamed on after dawn.
Men go crazy this way . . . not I. All's black again,
But the dream was sweet. Black, black, black. Ah,"
He said to the door, "keep still!"

                                    The knocking ceased
And steps retreated. Suddenly his black anguish
Compelled him to kneel by the bed. "What shall I do?
Kill that woman? I've promised not to kill
Fly nor stinking beetle. Nor myself: that
Would be a little too easy, I am a murderer
But not a coward yet. Nothing, is hardest to do.
Oh, God show me a way. Nothing?" The prayer
And the attitude stiffened his nerves with self-contempt.
He ceased and stood up. "Nor this." Himself was responsible,
Himself must choose, himself must endure. He stood
And looked at the bed, remembering the sweet dream.

More steps came to the door and he drew it open
Before one knocked. Fera said "You are sick,
And I was afraid to come back alone. I brought
Concha Rosas." He looked from one to the other,–
"Both my vomits," he said gently. "I'll never
Send you away. This is something." She whispered to him:
"You are in danger. Everyone here . . . knows.
Ask Concha. If you shut yourself up they'll tell; they've been
    asked;
Only the fear of your face stops them.

Jesus Acanna was asked in Monterey
When he drove in the steers." Cawdor said gently:
"Stay here. I'll keep you with me both days and nights
For a live spark between the eye-lid and the eye.
What ails you to bring good news?" "I knew he was going mad.
Good news? Why, they'll not hang you. I'll be your perfect
Witness to keep you alive. Buried alive
While all the strength you're proud of rots and drops off,
And all the stupid and deceived mind
Tears itself into red strips behind gray
Stones and black iron. Where is it, San Quentin? Oh, kill yourself
    Cawdor.
You have no better hope." "I am all you say,
Blind, blind, blind dupe," he answered, "but not a coward
    yet." "My God,
Watch the man cling, Concha. Who'd ever think
That *his* was sweet to live? But it's not love of life,
It's terror of death." He was not listening. He looked
With softened anxious eyes at the bed, his lips
Moved, though he did not speak. She, not in mockery:
"What do you see?" "A face that I know perfectly
Was crushed—what day of the month is it?—three months
And certain days ago, to a red lump
Of sudden destruction: but can you see?—he smiles at me.
I know there is nothing there." Fera laughed, "Concha
Has scuttled away. *I* see his angry eyes
And tumbled light brown hair and bare strong shoulders . . ."
"Yes: his hair." ". . . when I ran in here at dawn,
He lifted himself in the bed like a white sea-lion
Out of the running wave. His breast was bare.
And it was smooth, it was like smooth grooved stone.
You caught me here in the room." Cawdor looked down
And smiled and trembled. "Perhaps if I hadn't come.
Perhaps if I hadn't come." "You were pitiful enough,"
She said, "before. We'd both like to think that.

No, he was straight and true and faithful as light.
Hard as crystal, there was not a spot to hold by.
We two are damned." She watched him shaking
And thought that now he would make some end; but he
Looked downward sideways and said "It has faded now.
You needn't wait, I'll never again do anything
Until I have thought and thought. I'll find a way."
He said in the door, "I thought the woman was with you."
"Concha? She scuttled: I told you." "No, you said nothing."

She followed. When they were on the stair they heard
George's revolver-shot that killed the eagle,
And the quick echo. Cawdor stopped on the stair
And looked at Fera's face. "Why did you turn
So strangely," she said, "what do you see? I fear
You have waited too long already and now your mind
Is helpless among many voices and ghosts.
Kill yourself, Cawdor, and be safe from that,
For soon it will be too late." He said drearily,
"Since you fooled me my ears and eyes have the trick.
But," with a burrowing motion of the head forward,
"I'm not deceived. Not deceived. . . . Who has Hood's rifle?"
"Ah," she answered, "old fox, that hole won't hide you.
He fired because you were coming at him to kill him:
Your guilt's no less." "I lost it," he said, "in the night in the oaks.
I've often looked there, he loved it." They went out-doors
Under the twisted cypress trees and Cawdor said,
"What were you saying? He fired in the air, not at me.
If you were full of eyes you'd find no fault in him."
Fera laughed out, and pointing at the oak on the hill:
"Hurrah, she's done it. That was the shot. Oh, well done Michal.
See if I always fail. The bird shut in a box
Was eating bitter meat for years and now it is blessed. I've been
    begging her

To make it blessed. Its arm was like mine." "Killed it? I'm sorry,"
    he said, "for Michal." Suddenly he ran
To the dim path and climbed. He shouted "George, George";
    his heavy voice and the echo of his voice battered
Upward between the walls of the canyon.

                                              He came to the shelf
    of earth, and hoarse with breathlessness: "More killing?
You dog, have you got Hood's gun?" Michal looked at his face
    with startled wet eyes, George did not speak
But held out the revolver in the flat of his hand. "I forgot that,"
    Cawdor said. "Oh Michal, you loved
This brave-eyed thing. You fed it for years." "It was unhappy,
    father." "By God, if you go killing
Unhappiness who'll be left in the houses? Forgive me," he said
    humbly, "I've much to bear." She, trembling:
"Why . . ." she wetted her lips with her tongue . . . "why did you
    ask about Hood's rifle, he wouldn't leave it?"
George, hastily: "His mind's on another matter. You told
    me to fix the branding-iron shafts . . ." Fera had come
Behind Cawdor, and driving her face like an axe between them:
    "Let him confess. He came to confess.
Listen to him for that will deliver his mind, thence he may win
Your eagle's quietness: we used to feel this cage like a black
    sun shining darkness on the canyon.
Now you've put out the sun, you've cured the sky with a gun-shot,
    nothing but a draggled feather-duster
Left in the cage. Let him confess." Cawdor said hoarsely: "I have
    learned that Hood was innocent. This woman
So angered me that I threatened his life in the night. I am dull
    and easy to lie to. Hood went away
Rather than quarrel with the fool his father; he left his rifle under
    my feet by the fire; I lost it;
If I could find it I'd keep it for him." "Ai," Fera cried sharply,
    "this is no good. Wait, that gray face

Will ripen by summer: you can't bear it forever. What
  did he use, his revolver? Even so little
A creature as that is a key to peace." Cawdor said, "Let
  me see it again." George clicked the cylinder
Out of the frame before he handed it to him. Cawdor took
  and returned it. "If I were weak enough
I could find ways, though I am not wise." He saw a knife-edged
  flake of chipped flint or chalcedony
On the earth at his feet; they stood by Fera's father's grave,
  and the spring rains had failed and not grassed it.
Cawdor picked up the Indian-wrought stone. "There were people
  here before us," he said, "and others will come
After our time. These poor flints were their knives, wherever
  you dig you find them, and now I forget
What we came up for. Why do you fix your eyes on me?
For I can neither imagine what I must do
Nor what I should say. You are like shadows." George said
  "Father:
Send this woman away. This is the bitter fountain, this is your
  sickness." "For the rifle," she answered,
"Acanna has it. Send me away: do: I've a pretty story for strangers,
  I'll bring back eyes
And dig for the old dog's hoard of bones." She said to Cawdor:
  "Now you've grown gentle, you can't eat meat,
But the others know we'd venison Thursday, Jesus Acanna killed
  it. He says that he got his rifle
In Monterey, have you seen the rifle, Michal? You country people
  have quick minds." "Oh, this is nothing,"
Cawdor groaned, "What does Hood want with a gun? He hunts
  no more.
However . . . do you see the sun?" George took his arm: "Come,
  let's go down." "Now it's due south," he answered,
"And men come home from the starved fields for food.
We'll go and ask him." George made a sign to Michal
So that she stayed behind when the others went down.

And Cawdor, seeing it: "That was well done. I see you now.
A moment ago you were like shadows of moths
When lamplight falls on the earth outside the window.
If I could have caught you I couldn't have held you. Send away
    sweet Fera?
What should we do without her?" She said: "That flint
Came from an old man's grave you used to despise
For his great weakness; he was the only mind in this ditch;
But now you don't. What's it for, to nick an artery?"
"It is hard," he answered, "and pleasant in the hand.
Last night I threw my knife out of the window
For fear it might use itself of its own accord.
I'd a good dream."

                    He saw Acanna among the cypresses
And called him with the old strength of his voice. "I hear that
    you've got Hood's rifle, you found it in the little oaks
Near by the Rock. Oh, keep it," he said, "keep it. That's nothing.
    Kill all the deer for Hood has quit hunting,
Buck, fawn and doe. They say they have foot-and-mouth disease
And carry it over the mountain. But if you see a white doe,
That's the worst kind. Cut out her tongue when she drops,
It's poison. . . . You know that I killed him.
You all know it. George knows it. You've been whispering
    for long,
Watching my face. You've been staunch and not told
For askings: but that was wrong, it makes you accessory.
Now you must ride and tell, don't stay for dinner.
Get meat in the house and eat on the road, for now
I've confessed: if you don't tell you'll be in the same
Sickness with Cawdor. Go. Go." He pushed by him,
And Acanna stood all twisted, as Cawdor's hands
Had left him, unable to move, looking for guidance. At length
George twitched his dead-white face and answered: "Go on.
Do what he says. He has chosen." While they stood, Cawdor

Faced the hill so that his back was toward them and drove
The point of the flint through fold and flesh of each eye,
Drawing sidewise on the stroke, so that his sight
Was burst, and blood and water ran down to his feet.
He did not groan, but Fera saw the red stream
Fall by some yellow flowers. She cried "Have you done
Wisely at last? Not with that chip?" He groaned then,
But answered nothing. Then George ran to him and saw
The bitter thing he had done, and moved with sudden
Ungovernable pity thrust the revolver
Into his hand. Cawdor said: "What's this? Oh,
This thing. Keep it for cage-birds.
We have other plans. The decent girl my pleasant companion
Has promised to lead me by the hand up to the Rock
And prove our wings." But Fera staggered and said,
Her arms hanging straight down, head drooped, and knees
Bent like weak age: "I am broken. It is finished."
She covered her eyes against him. "My courage is past.
I have always failed." He said, "I'd not have flown down.
I meant to sit up there and think my old thoughts
Until they come to-morrow and take me. It was mere indulgence.
These punishments are a pitiful self-indulgence.
I'd not the strength to do nothing.

                    Be kind to Michal:
But spring's weeping-time. Oh, George it was her face
I fell into this darkness to hide myself from.
But when I am taken from the sight of my mountain
It is better to have no eyes. Has Acanna gone?
Your droughty hay-harvest will be a thin sight."
He extended his hands. "Lead me, whoever is here,
Into the house. My head is full of sharp lightnings
And the ground streams and falls under my feet."

Medea

First Act

The Nurse comes from the doorsteps toward the front of the stage.

THE NURSE
I wish the long ship Argo had never passed that perilous channel
    between the Symplegades,
I wish the pines that made her mast and her oars still waved
    in the wind on Mount Pelion, and the gray fishhawk
Still nested in them, the great adventurers had never voyaged
Into the Asian sunrise to the shores of morning for the Golden
    Fleece.

        For then my mistress Medea
Would never have seen Jason nor loved and saved him, nor cut
    herself off from home to come with him
Into this country of the smiling chattering Greeks and the roofs
    of Corinth: over which I see evil
Hang like a cloud. For she is not meek but fierce, and the daughter
    of a king.

        Yet at first all went well.
The folk of Corinth were kind to her, they were proud of her beauty,
    and Jason loved her. Happy is the house
Where the man and the woman love and are faithful.

113

Now all is
changed; all is black hatred. For Jason
Has turned from her; he calls the old bond a barbarian mating,
    not a Greek marriage; he has cast her off
And wedded the yellow-haired child of Creon, the ruler here.
He wants worldly advantage, fine friends,
And a high place in Corinth. For these he is willing to cast Medea
    like a harlot, and betray the children
That she has borne him. He is not wise, I think.

But Medea
Lies in the house, broken with pain and rage, she will neither
    eat nor drink, except her own tears,
She turns her face toward the earth, remembering her father's
    house and her native land, which she abandoned
For the love of this man: who now despises her.
And if I try to speak comfort to her she only stares at me, great
    eyes like stones. She is like a stone on the shore
Or a wave of the sea, and I think she hates
Even her children. She is learning what it is to be a foreigner,
    cast out, alone and despised.
She will never learn to be humble, she will never learn to drink
    insult
Like harmless water. O I'm in terror of her: whether she'll thread
    a knife through her own heart,
Or whether she'll hunt the bridegroom and his new bride,
    or what more dreadful evil stalks in the forest
Of her dark mind. I know that Jason would have been wiser
    to tempt a lioness, or naked-handed
Steal the whelps of a tiger.
    [She sees Medea's sons coming with their tutor.]
                Here come the happy children. Little
    they know
Of their mother's grief.

THE TUTOR *entering with the two little boys*
                    Old servant of my lady, why do you stand
out here, keeping watch in solitude
With those grim eyes? Is it some trouble of your own that
    you are lamenting? I should think Medea
Would need your care.

THE NURSE
It is all one to Medea, whether I am there or here. Yes, it is mine.
My trouble. My lady's grief is my grief. And it has hurt me
So that I had to come out and speak it to the earth and sky.

THE TUTOR
                                                    Is she

still in that deep despair?

THE NURSE
                    You are lucky,
Old watchdog of Jason's boys. I envy you,
You do not see her. This evil is not declining, it is just at dawn.
    I dread the lion-eyed
Glare of its noon.

THE TUTOR
            Is she so wrought? Yet neither you nor Medea
Knows the latest and worst.

THE NURSE
                    What? What?

THE TUTOR
                                        I shouldn't have spoken.
No, it is nothing.

THE NURSE

        Tell me the truth, old man. You and I are two
slaves, we can trust each other,
We can keep secrets.

THE TUTOR

        I heard them saying—when we walked
beside the holy fountain Peirene,
Where the old men sit in the sun on the stone benches—they
were saying that Creon, the lord of this land,
Intends to drive out Medea and the children with her, these
innocent boys, out of this house
And out of Corinth, and they must wander through the wild
world
Homeless and helpless.

THE NURSE

        I don't believe it. Ah, no! Jason may hate
the mother, but he would hardly
Let his sons be cast out.

THE TUTOR

        Well . . . he has made a new alliance.
He is not a friend of this house.

THE NURSE

If this were true!—Listen: I hear her voice. Take the children
away, keep them away from her.
Take them to the other door. Quickly.

*[They go out, toward a rear door of the house. The Nurse looks
after them, wringing her hands.]*

116

MEDEA *within the house. She is Asiatic and laments loudly.*
Death. Death is my wish. For myself, my enemies, my children.
Destruction.
That's the word. Grind, crush, burn. Destruction. Ai . . .. Ai . . ..

THE NURSE *wringing her hands*
This is my terror:
To hear her always harking back to the children, like a fierce
    hound at fault. O unhappy one,
They're not to blame.

MEDEA *within*
                    If any god hears me: let me die. Ah, rotten,
    rotten, rotten: death is the only
Water to wash this dirt.

[*Chorus is coming in, by twos and threes, but the Nurse does not
yet notice them. She is intent on Medea's cries and her own
thoughts.*]

THE NURSE
                    Oh, it's a bad thing
To be born of high race, and brought up wilful and powerful
    in a great house, unruled
And ruling many: for then if misfortune comes it is unendurable,
    it drives you mad. I say that poor people
Are happier: the little commoners and humble people, the poor
    in spirit: they can lie low
Under the wind and live: while the tall oaks and cloud-raking
    mountain pines go mad in the storm,
Writhe, groan and crash. This is the wild and terrible justice
    of God: it brings on great persons

The great disasters.
*[She becomes aware of the women who have come in, and is startled
from her reverie.]*
What do you want?

FIRST WOMAN

I hear her crying again:
it is dreadful.

SECOND WOMAN

Her lamentation.
She is beautiful and deep in grief: we couldn't help coming.

THIRD WOMAN

We are friends of this house and its trouble hurts us.

THE NURSE

You are right, friends, it is not a home. It is broken.
A house of grief and of weeping.

MEDEA *within*

Hear me, God, let me die. What
I need: all dead, all dead, all dead,
Under the great cold stones. For a year and a thousand years
    and another thousand: cold as the stones, cold,
But noble again, proud, straight and silent, crimson-cloaked
In the blood of our wounds.

FIRST WOMAN

O shining sky, divine earth,
Harken not to the song that this woman sings.
It is not her mind's music, her mind is not here.
She does not know what she prays for.
Pain and wrath are the singers.

118

SECOND WOMAN
                              Unhappy one,
Never pray for death, never pray for death,
He is here all too soon.
He strikes from the clear sky like a hawk,
He hides behind green leaves, or he waits
Around the corner of the wall.
O never pray for death, never pray for death—
Because that prayer will be answered.

MEDEA *The rise and fall of her voice indicate that she is prowling*
  back and forth beyond the doorway, like a caged animal.
I know poisons. I know the bright teeth of steel. I know fire.
  But I will not be mocked by my enemies,
And I will not endure pity. Pity and contempt are sister
  and brother, twin-born. I will not die tamely.
I will not allow blubber-eyed pity, nor contempt either, to snivel
  over the stones of my tomb.
I am not a Greek woman.

THIRD WOMAN
                            No, a barbarian woman from savage
  Colchis, at the bitter end
Of the Black Sea. Does she boast of that?

SECOND WOMAN
                                    She doesn't know what
  she is saying.

MEDEA *in the house*
Poisons. Death-magic. The sharp sword. The hemp rope.
Death-magic. Death . . ..

SECOND WOMAN
                        I hate Jason, who made this sorrow.

FIRST WOMAN   *to the Nurse*

Old and honored servant of a great house, do you think it is wise
To leave your lady alone in there, except perhaps a few slaves,
    building that terrible acropolis
Of deadly thoughts? We Greeks believe that solitude is very
    dangerous, great passions grow into monsters
In the dark of the mind; but if you share them with loving
    friends they remain human, they can be endured.
I think you ought to persuade Medea to come from the dark
    dwelling and speak with us, before her heart breaks,
Or she does harm to herself. She has lived among us, we've
    learned to love her, we'd gladly tell her so.
It might comfort her spirit.

THE NURSE

                          Do you think so? She wouldn't listen.
    —Oh, oh, she is coming!
Speak carefully to her; make your words a soft music.

*[Medea comes through the doorway, propping herself against
one of the pillars, and stands staring.]*

THE NURSE

Oh, my dear, my poor child.   *[She hurries toward Medea.]*

SECOND WOMAN   *whispering*

They say she is dangerous. Look at her eyes.

FIRST WOMAN

She is a witch, but not evil. She can make old men young again:
    she did it for Jason's father.

THIRD WOMAN

All the people of her country are witches. They know about drugs
    and magic. They are savages, but they have a wild wisdom.

120

SECOND WOMAN
Poor soul, it hasn't helped this one much.

MEDEA *She does not see the gaping and whispering women.*
I will look at the light of the sun, this last time. I wish from that
    blue sky the white wolf of lightning
Would leap, and burst my skull and my brain, and like a burning
    babe cling to these breasts . . ..
[She checks and looks fiercely at the women below.]
Someone is here?
    *[Her hostile eyes range back and forth; she sees the women clearly
    now, and assumes full self-control. Her voice is cautious and
    insincere.]*   I did not know I had visitors. . . . Women of Corinth,
If anything has been spoken too loudly here, consider
That I believed I was alone; and I have some provocation. You've
    come—let me suppose
With love and sympathy—to peer at my sorrow. I understand
    well enough
That nothing is ever private in a Greek city; whoever withholds
    anything
Is thought sullen or proud . . .
    [with irony]   undemocratic
I think you call it. This is not always just, but we know that
    justice, at least on earth,
Is a name, not a fact; and as for me, I wish to avoid any appearance
Of being . . . proud. Of what? Of affliction? I will show you my
    naked heart. You know that my lord Jason
Has left me and made a second marriage, with the bright-haired
    child
Of wealth and power. I too was a child of power, but not in this
    country; and I spent my power
For love of Jason. I poured it out before him like water, I made
    him drink it like wine. I gave him
Success and fame; I saved him his precious life; not once, many
    times. You may have heard what I did for him:

I betrayed my father for him, I killed my brother to save
    him; I made my own land to hate me forever;
And I fled west with Jason in the Greek ship, under the thunder
    of the sail, weeping and laughing,
That huge journey through the Black Sea and the Bosphorus,
    where the rocks clang together, through the Sea of
    Marmora,
And through the Hellespont, watched by the spearmen of wealthy
    Troy, and home to Greek water: his home, my exile,
My endless exile. And here I have loved him and borne
    him sons; and this . . . man . . .
Has left me and taken Creon's daughter, to enjoy her fortune,
    and put aside her soft yellow hair
And kiss her young mouth.
    [Medea stands rigid, struggling for self-control.]

FIRST WOMAN
She is terrible. Stone with stone eyes.

SECOND WOMAN
Look: the foam-flake on her lip, that flickers with her breathing.

THIRD WOMAN
She is pitiable: she is under great injuries.

MEDEA *low-voiced*
I do not know what other women . . . I do not know how much
    a Greek woman
Will endure. The people of my race are somewhat rash
    and intemperate. As for me, I want simply to die.
But Jason is not to smile at his bride over my grave, nor that
    great man Creon
Hang wreaths and make a feast-day in Corinth. Or let the wreaths
    be bright blinding fire, and the songs a high wailing,
And the wine, blood.

122

FIRST WOMAN
                    Daughter of sorrow, beware.
It is dangerous to dream of wine, it is worse
To speak of wailing or blood:
For the images that the mind makes
Find a way out, they work into life.

MEDEA
                              Let them work into life!

FIRST WOMAN
There are evils that cannot be cured by evil.
Patience remains, and the gods watch all.

MEDEA *dully, without hope*
Let them watch my enemies go down in blood.

SECOND WOMAN
                                        Medea, beware!
Some great person is coming.—It is Creon himself!

THIRD WOMAN
Creon is coming.

THE NURSE
                    He is dark with anger. O my lady . . . my child
. . . bend in this wind,
And not be broken!

[*Creon comes in, with men attending him. The women move to one side. He speaks to Medea, with an angry gesture toward chorus.*]

CREON
You have admirers, I see. Abate your pride: these people
    will not be with you where you are going.

123

[A pause. Medea does not answer. Creon brings his wrath under control.]

Medea, woman of the stone forehead and hate-filled eyes: I have
    made my decision. I have decided
That you must leave this land at once and go into banishment,
    you with your children. I intend to remove
A root of disturbance out of the soil of Corinth. I am here
    to see to it. I will not return home
Until it is done.

MEDEA
           You mean . . . banishment?

CREON
                         Exile: banishment:
go where you may, Medea, but here
You abide no more.

MEDEA
           . . . I with my children?

CREON
                       I will not take them
away from you.

MEDEA
         Because we have suffered evil
We are to suffer more evil. Death was my wish.

CREON
                      Ha? Words. You'll
not be hindered: you can have death
While there are ropes to hang by or waves to drown in. Only
    make haste
And leave this land.

124

MEDEA

          The children, my lord . . ..
[*Her lips move angrily, but the voice is not heard.*]

CREON

                              What are you
muttering?

MEDEA

Nothing . . . I am praying to my gods for wisdom.
And you for mercy. My sons are still very young, tender
     and helpless. You know, my lord,
What exile means—to wander with fear and famine for guide
     and driver, through all the wild winter storms
And the rage of the sun; and beg a bread-crust and be derided;
     pelted with stones in the villages,
Held a little lower than the scavenger dogs, kicked, scorned
     and slaved—the children, my lord,
Are Jason's children. Your chosen friend, I believe, and now
Even closer bound. And as for me, your servant, O master
     of Corinth, what have I done? Why
Must I be cast?

CREON

          I will tell you frankly: because you nourish
     rancorous ill will toward persons
Whom I intend to protect: I send you out before you've time
     to do harm here. And you are notorious
For occult knowledge: sorcery, poisons, magic. Men say you can
     even sing down the moon from heaven,
And make the holy stars to falter and run backward, against
     the purpose
And current of nature. Ha? As to that I know not: I know you are
     dangerous. You threaten my daughter: you have to go.

                                        125

MEDEA

But I wish her well, my lord! I wish her all happiness. I hope that
Jason may be as kind to her
As . . . to me.

CREON *fiercely*
That is your wish?

MEDEA

I misspoke. I thought of . . . old
days . . . . *[She seems to weep.]*

CREON
I acknowledge, Medea,
That you have some cause for grief. I all the more must guard
against your dark wisdom and bitter heart.

MEDEA

You misjudge me cruelly. It is true that I have some knowledge
of drugs and medicines: I can sometimes cure sickness:
Is that a crime? These dark rumors, my lord,
Are only the noise of popular gratitude. You must have observed
it often: if any person
Knows a little more than the common man, the people suspect
him. If he brings a new talent,
How promptly the hateful whispers begin. But you are not a
common man, lord of Corinth, you
Will not fear knowledge.

CREON
No. Nor change my decision. I am here
to see you leave this house and the city:
And not much time. Move quickly, gather your things and go. I pity
you, Medea,
But you must go.

126

MEDEA
         You pity me? You . . . pity me?
[She comes close to him, wild with rage.]
I will endure a dog's pity or a wart-grown toad's. May God who
hears me . . . . We shall see in the end
Who's to be pitied.

CREON   *shocked, recovering his dignity*
                 This is good. This is what I desire. Unmask
the livid face of your hatred
And I see whom I deal with. Serpent and wolf: a wolf from Asia:
   I'd rather have you rage now
Than do harm later. Now. Medea: out of here.
Before my men drive you out.

MEDEA   *controls her fury, then speaks.*
                    You see a woman driven half
   mad with sorrow, laboring to save
Her little children. No wolf, my lord. And though I was born
   in far-off Asia: call that misfortune,
Not vice. The races of Asia are human too,
As the bright Greeks are. And our hearts are as brittle: if you hurt
   us we cry. And we have children and love them,
As Greeks do. You have a daughter, sir—

CREON
                        Yes, and I'll keep her safe
of your female hatred: therefore I send you
Out of this land.

MEDEA
         It is not true, I am not jealous, I never hated her.
Jealous for the sake of Jason? I am far past wanting Jason, my lord.
   You took him and gave him to her,

And I will say you did well, perhaps wisely. Your daughter
    is loved by all: she is beautiful: if I were near her
I should soon love her.

CREON

                         You can speak sweetly enough, you can
    make honey in your mouth like a brown bee
When it serves your turn.

MEDEA

                         Not honey: the truth.

CREON

                                        Trust you or not,
    you are going out of this country, Medea.
What I decide is fixed; it is like the firm rocks of Acrocorinth,
    which neither earthquake can move
Nor a flood of tears melt. Make ready quickly: I have a guest
    in my house. I should return to him.

THE NURSE *comes beside Medea and speaks to her.*
What guest? O my lady, ask him
Who is the guest? If powerful and friendly
He might be a refuge to us in bitter exile . . .

MEDEA *pays no attention to her. Kneels to Creon.*
I know that your will is granite. But even on the harsh face
    of a granite mountain some flowers of mercy
May grow in season. Have mercy on my little sons, Creon,
Though there is none for me.
    [She reaches to embrace his knees. He steps backward from her.]

CREON

                         How long, woman? This is decided;
    done; finished.

128

MEDEA   *Rising from her knees, turns half away from him.*
                    I am not a beggar.
I will not trouble you. I shall not live long.
    [She turns to him again.]
Sire: grant me a few hours yet, one day to prepare in, one little day
Before I go out of Corinth forever.

CREON
                                        What? No! I told you. The day
        is today, Medea, this day.
And the hour is now.

MEDEA
                    There are no flowers on this mountain:
        not one violet, not one anemone.
Your face, my lord, is like flint.—If I could find the right words,
        if some god would lend me a touch of eloquence,
I'd show you my heart. I'd lift it out of my breast and turn it over
        in my hands, you'd see how pure it is
Of any harm or malice toward you or your household.
    [She holds out her hands to him.]   Look at it:
        not a speck: look, my lord. They call mercy
The jewel of kings. I am praying
To you as to one of the gods: destroy us not utterly. To go out with
        no refuge, nothing prepared,
Is plain death: I would rather kill myself quickly and here.
        If I had time but to ask the slaves
And strolling beggars where to go, how to live: and I must gather
        some means: one or two jewels
And small gold things I have, to trade them for bread and goat's
        milk. Wretched, wretched, wretched I am,
I and my boys.
    [She kneels again.]
                    I beseech you, Creon,

By the soft yellow hair and cool smooth forehead and the white
    knees
Of that young girl who is now Jason's bride: lend me this inch
    of time: one day—half a day,
For this one is now half gone—and I will go my sad course
    and vanish in the morning quietly as dew
That drops on the stones at dawn and is dry at sunrise.
    You will never again be troubled by any word
Or act of mine. And this I pray you for your dear child's sake.
    Oh Creon, what is half a day
In all the rich years of Corinth?

CREON
                            I will think of it. I am no tyrant.
I have been merciful to my own hurt, many times. Even to myself
    I seem to be foolish
If I grant you this thing . . . .. No, Medea,
I will not grant it.

*[She has been kneeling with bowed head. Silently she raises
her imploring face toward him.]*

                            Well . . . .. We shall watch you: as a hawk does
    a viper. What harm could she do
In the tail of one day? A ruler ought to be ruthless, but
    I am not. I am a fool
In my own eyes, whatever the world may think. I can be gruff
    with warriors, a woman weeping
Floods me off course.—Take it, then. Make your preparations.
But if tomorrow's sun shines on you here—Medea, you die.
    . . . Enough words. Thank me not. I want my hands
Washed of this business.

*[He departs quickly, followed by his men. Medea rises from
her knees.]*

MEDEA
                    I will thank you.
And the whole world will hear of it.

FIRST WOMAN
I have seen this man's arrogance, I watched and heard him.
I am of Corinth, and I say that Corinth
Is not well ruled.

SECOND WOMAN
The city where even a woman, even a foreigner,
Suffers unjustly the rods of power
Is not well ruled.

FIRST WOMAN
Unhappy Medea, what haven, what sanctuary, where will
     you wander?
Which of the gods, Medea,
Drives you through waves of woe, the mooring broken,
     the hawsers and the anchor-head,
Hopeless from harbor?

MEDEA
                    ... This man ... this barking dog ... this
     gulled fool ... gods of my father's country,
You saw me low on my knees before the great dog of Corinth;
     humble, holding my heart in my hands
For a dog to bite—break this dog's teeth!
                                        Women: it is a bitter
     thing to be a woman.
A woman is weak for warfare, she must use cunning. Men boast
     their battles: I tell you this, and we know it:
It is easier to stand in battle three times, in the front line,
     in the stabbing fury, than to bear one child.

And a woman, they say, can do no good but in childbirth.
    It may be so. She can do evil, she can do evil.
I wept before that tall dog, I wept my tears before him, I degraded
    my knees to him, I gulled and flattered him:
O triple fool, he has given me all that I needed: a little time,
    a space of time. Death is dearer to me
Than what I am now; and if today by sunset the world has not
    turned, and turned sharp too—let your dog Creon
Send two or three slaves to kill me and a cord to strangle
    me: I will stretch out
My throat to it. But I have a bitter hope, women. I begin
    to see light
Through the dark wood, between the monstrous trunks of the trees,
    at the end of the tangled forest an eyehole,
A pin-point of light: I shall not die perhaps
As a pigeon dies. Nor like an innocent lamb, that feels a hand
    on its head and looks up from the knife
To the man's face and dies.—No, like some yellow-eyed beast
    that has killed its hunters let me lie down
On the hounds' bodies and the broken spears.—Then how to strike
    them? What means to use? There are so many
Doors through which painful death may glide in and catch . . .
    which one, which one?

[*She stands meditating. The Nurse comes from behind her and speaks
to the first woman of the chorus.*]

THE NURSE

                        Tell me: do you know what guest
Is in Creon's house?

FIRST WOMAN

                What?—Oh. An Athenian ship came from
the north last night: it is Aegeus,
The lord of Athens.

132

THE NURSE

Aegeus! My lady knows him: I believe he will
help us. Some god has brought him here,
Some savior god.

FIRST WOMAN

He is leaving, I think, today.

THE NURSE *hobbling back toward Medea*

My lady! Lord
Aegeus
Is here in Corinth, Creon's guest. Aegeus of Athens.

[*Medea looks at her silently, without attention.*]

If you will
see him and speak him fairly,
We have a refuge.

MEDEA

I have things in my hand to do. Be quiet.

THE NURSE

Oh,
listen to me!
You are driven out of Corinth, you must find shelter. Aegeus
of Athens is here.

[*Medea turns from her and moves to re-enter the house. The Nurse
catches at her clothing, servile but eager, slave and mother
at the same time.*]

MEDEA *angrily turning on her*
What's that to me?

133

THE NURSE

I lifted you in my arms when you were . . . this long. I gave
you milk from these breasts, that are now dead leaves.
I saw the little beautiful body straighten and grow tall:
Oh . . . child . . . almost my child . . . how can I
Not try to save you? Life is better than death—

MEDEA

Not now.

THE NURSE

Time's

running out!

MEDEA

I have time. Oh, I have time.
It would be good to sit here a thousand years and think of nothing
But the deaths of three persons.

THE NURSE

Ai! There's no hope then.
Ai, child, if you could do this red thing you dream of, all Corinth
Would pour against you.

MEDEA

After my enemies are punished and I have
heard the last broken moan—Corinth?
What's that? I'll sleep well. I am alone against all; and so weary
That it is pitiful.

*[The Nurse stands wringing her hands. Medea goes slowly
up to the door of the house. Some of the Corinthian women
are watching her; others gaze into the distance.]*

134

FIRST WOMAN
        Look: who is coming? I see the sunlight glitter
on lanceheads.

SECOND WOMAN
Oh, it is Jason!

THIRD WOMAN
Jason! Medea's worst enemy, who should have been
Her dearest protector.

*[Medea leans wearily against one of the pillars of the doorway,
her back to the stage, unconscious of what they are saying.
Jason enters in haste, followed by armed attendants, and speaks
angrily.]*

JASON
        What business have you here, you women
Clustered like buzzing bees at the hive-door?
Where is Medea?

*[They do not answer for a moment, but look involuntarily toward
Medea, and Jason sees her. She jerks and stiffens at the sound
of his voice, but does not turn.]*

FIRST WOMAN *pointing*
        There: mourning for what you have done.

JASON
                                        Ha?
What she has done.
Not I. Not by my will she and my sons are exiled.

[Medea slowly turns and faces him, her head high, rigid with inner violence.]

MEDEA

Is there another dog here?

JASON

So, Medea,
You have once more affronted and insulted the head of Corinth.
    This is not the first time
I've seen what a fool anger is. You might have lived here happily,
    secure and honored—I hoped you would—
By being just a little decently respectful toward those in power.
    Instead, you had to go mad with anger
And talk yourself into exile. To me it matters little what
    you say about me, but rulers are sensitive.
Time and again I've smoothed down Creon's indignation, then
    you like a madwoman, like a possessed imbecile,
Wag your head and let the words flow again; you never cease
From speaking evil against him and his family. So now—you've
    got it. Call yourself lucky, Medea,
Not to get worse than exile. In spite of all this, I have your interest
    at heart and am here to help you.
Exile's a bitter business, I want to make some provision
    for you. I wish you no harm,
Although you hate me.
    [He waits for her to speak, but she is silent. He continues:]
                    And in particular the children; my sons;
    our sons.—You might have been decent enough
To have thought of our sons.

MEDEA *slowly*
                    Did you consider them
When you betrayed this house?

136

JASON
                              Certainly I considered them.
It was my hope that they would grow up here,
And I, having married power, could protect and favor them.
      And if perhaps, after many years, I become
Dynast of Corinth—for that is Creon's desire, to make me his heir—
      our sons
Would have been a king's sons . . . . I hope to help them, wherever
      they go: but now of course must look forward
To younger children.

      MEDEA *trembling*
                              Ah . . . it's enough. Something might happen.
It is . . . likely that . . . something might happen
To the bride and the marriage.

      JASON
                              I'll guard against it. But evidently
Creon is right to be rid of you.

      MEDEA
Have you finished now? I thought I would let you speak
      on and spread out your shamelessness
Before these women: the way a Tyrian trader unrolls his rare
      fabrics: "Do you like it, ladies?" It is the
Dog's daughter's husband. It is a brave person: it has finally
      got up its courage—with a guard of spears—
To come and look me in the face.
                              O Jason: how have you pulled
      me down
To this hell of vile thoughts? I did not use to talk like a common
      woman. I loved you once:
And I am ashamed of it: but there are some things
That ought to be remembered by you and me. That blue day when
      we drove through the Hellespont

Into Greek sea, and the great-shouldered heroes were singing
    at the oars, and those birds flying
Through the blown foam: that day was too fine I suppose
For Creon's daughter's man to remember—but you might
    remember
Whether I cheated my father for you and tamed the fire-breathing
Brazen-hoofed bulls; and whether I saved your life in the field
    of the teeth; and you might remember
Whether I poisoned the great serpent and got you the Golden
    Fleece; and fled with you, and killed my brother
When he pursued us, making myself abominable
In my own home; and then in yours I got your enemy Pelias
    hacked to death
By his own daughters' hands—whatever these fine Corinthian
    friends of yours
May say against my rapid and tricky wisdom: you it has served,
You it has served well: here are five times, if I counted right—
    and all's not counted—
That your adventure would have been dusty death
If I'd not saved you—but now you think that your adventures
    are over; you are safe and high placed in Corinth,
And will need me no more.
                          It is a bit of a dog, isn't it, women?
    It is well qualified
To sleep with the dog's daughter. But for me, Jason, me driven
    by the hairy snouts from the quadruped marriage-bed,
What refuge does your prudent kindness advise? Shall I fly home
    to Colchis—
To put my neck in the coil of a knotted rope, for the crimes
I served you with? Or shall I go and kneel to the daughters
    of Pelias? They would indeed be happy
To lay their hands on my head: holding the very knives
    and the cleavers
That carved their sire. The world is a little closed to me, ah?
By the things I have done for you.

[Meanwhile the Nurse has come forward on the stage, and stands this side of chorus, listening, wringing her hands. Now she speaks.]

THE NURSE

                              I'll go to the palace
And seek for Aegeus. There is no other hope.
[She hurries out in that direction.]

JASON *slowly*

                              I see, Medea,
You have been a very careful merchant of benefits. You forget
    none, you keep a strict reckoning. But—
Some little things that I on my side have done for you
Ought to be in the books too: as, for example, that I carried you
Out of the dirt and superstition of Asiatic Colchis into the rational
Sunlight of Greece, and the marble music of the Greek temples:
    is that no benefit? And I have brought you
To meet the first minds of our time, and to speak as an equal
    with the great heroes and the rulers of cities:
Is that no benefit? And now—this grievous thing that you hate
    me for:
That I have married Creon's young daughter, little Creüsa:
    do you think I did it like a boy or a woman,
Out of blind passion? I did it to achieve power here; and I'd have
    used that power to protect
You and our sons, but your jealous madness has muddled
    everything. And finally:
As to those acts of service you so loudly boast—whom do I thank
    for them? I thank divine Venus, the goddess
Who makes girls fall in love. You did them because you had to do
    them; Venus compelled you; I
Enjoyed her favor. A man dares things, you know, he makes
    his adventure
In the cold eye of death; and if the gods care for him

They appoint an instrument to save him; if not, he dies. You were
that instrument.

MEDEA
Here it is: the lowest.
The obscene dregs; the slime and the loathing; the muddy bottom
of a mouthed cup: when a scoundrel begins
To invoke the gods. You had better go, Jason. Vulgarity
Is a contagious disease; and in a moment what could I do but spit
at you like a peasant, or curse you
Like a drunken slave? You had better take yourself back to . . .
"Little Creüsa."

JASON
I came to help you and save you if possible.

MEDEA
Your help
Is not wanted. Go. Go.

JASON
If I could see my boys . . ..

MEDEA
Go quickly.

JASON
Yours
the regret then.
[Exit.]

[Watching him go, Medea strokes her wrist and hand to the tips
of the spread fingers, as if she were scraping off slime.]

140

MEDEA

This is it. I did not surely know it: loathing is all. This flesh
He has touched and fouled. These hands that wrought
    for him, these knees
That ran his errands. This body that took his . . . what they call love,
    and made children of it. If I could peel off
The flesh, the children, the memory . . ..
    [Again she scarifies one hand with the other. She looks at her hand.]
                                    Poor misused hand: poor
    defiled arm: your bones
Are not unshapely. If I could tear off the flesh and be bones;
    naked bones;
Salt-scoured bones on the shore
At home in Colchis . . ..
    [She stands staring, thinking of home perhaps.]

FIRST CORINTHIAN WOMAN

God keep me from fire and the hunger of the sword,
Save me from the hateful sea and the jagged lightning,
And the violence of love.

SECOND WOMAN

A little love is a joy in the house,
A little fire is a jewel against frost and darkness.

FIRST WOMAN

A great love is a fire
That burns the beams of the roof.
The doorposts are flaming and the house falls.
A great love is a lion in the cattle-pen,
The herd goes mad, the heifers run bawling
And the claws are in their flanks.
Too much love is an armed robber in the treasury,
He has killed the guards and he walks in blood.

SECOND WOMAN
And now I see the black end,
The end of great love, and God save me from it:
The unburied horror, the unbridled hatred,
The vultures tearing a corpse:
God keep me clean of those evil beaks.

THIRD WOMAN
What is she doing, that woman,
Staring like stone, staring?
Oh, she has moved now.

MEDEA
Annihilation. The word is pure music: annihilation. To annihilate
    the past—
Is not possible: but its fruit in the present . . .
Can be nipped off. Am I to look in my sons' eyes
And see Jason's forever? How could I endure the endless
    defilement, those lives
That mix Jason and me? Better to be clean
Bones on the shore. Bones have no eyes at all, how could they
    weep? White bones
On the Black Sea shore . . . .
                            Oh, but that's far. Not yet. Corinth
    must howl first.
    [She stands meditating.]

FIRST WOMAN
The holy fountains flow up from the earth,
The smoke of sacrifice flows up from the earth,
The eagle and the wild swan fly up from the earth,
Righteousness also
Has flown up from the earth to the feet of God.
It is not here, but up there; peace and pity are departed;

Hatred is here; hatred is heavy, it clings to the earth.
Love blows away, hatred remains.

SECOND WOMAN
Women hate war, but men will wage it again.
Women may hate their husbands, and sons their fathers,
But women will never hate their own children.

FIRST WOMAN
But as for me, I will do good to my husband,
I will love my sons and daughters, and adore the gods.

MEDEA
If I should go into the house with a sharp knife
To the man and his bride . . .
Or if I could fire the room they sleep in, and hear them
Wake in the white of the fire, and cry to each other, and howl
    like dogs,
And howl and die . . .
But I might fail; I might be cut down first;
The knife might turn in my hand, or the fire not burn,
    and my enemies could laugh at me.
No: I have subtler means, and more deadly cruel; I have
    my dark art
That fools call witchcraft. Not for nothing I have worshipped
    the wild gray goddess that walks in the dark, the wise one,
The terrible one, the sweet huntress, flower of night, Hecate,
In my house at my hearth.

THE NURSE   has entered, and hurries toward Medea.
                    My lady: he was leaving Creon's
door: he is coming.

[Medea pays no attention; the Nurse kneels, catches her hand.]

Aegeus is coming!
The power of Athens.

MEDEA

I will not see him. Go back and tell him so.

[The Nurse retreats behind chorus. Medea prays:]

Ancient Goddess to whom I and my people
Make the sacrifice of black lambs and black female hounds,
Holy one, haunter of cross-roads, queen of night, Hecate,
Help me now: to remember in my mind the use of the venomous
    fire, the magic song,
And the sharp gems.
[She sits on the steps in deep thought.]

*[Aegeus comes in, with attendants. His servants are not armed;
they have a look of travel and the sea.]*

FIRST CORINTHIAN WOMAN
He is here, Medea.
Athens is here.

[Medea pays no attention.]

AEGEUS *comes near to her.*
Medea, rejoice! There is no fairer greeting from
friend to friend.

[She ignores him. He speaks more loudly.]

Hail and rejoice, Medea!

[She lifts her head and stares at him.]

144

MEDEA

"Rejoice?" It may be so. It may be I
shall . . . rejoice
Before the sun sets.

AEGEUS

Medea! What has happened to you?

MEDEA

Nothing.

AEGEUS
Your eyes are cavernous!
And your mouth twitches.

MEDEA

Nothing: I am quite well: fools trouble
me.—Where are you travelling from,
Aegeus?

AEGEUS
From Delphi, where I went to consult
The ancient oracle of Apollo.

MEDEA *abstractedly*

Oh . . . Delphi . . . Did you get a
good answer?

AEGEUS
An obscure one.
Some god or other has made me unable to beget a child: that
    is my trouble: but the oracle
Never gives plain responses. I tell you these things because
    you are skilled in mysteries, and you might help me
To the god's meaning.

145

MEDEA *wearily*
                    You want a child! What did Apollo
Say to you?

AEGEUS
        That I must not unloose the hanging foot
of the wineskin until I return
To the hearth of my fathers.

MEDEA *without interest, but understanding the anatomical*
reference   The hanging foot of the wineskin.
You have never had a child?

AEGEUS
                            No.
And it is bitterness.

MEDEA
                But when misfortune comes it is bitter to have
children, and watch their starlike
Faces grow dim to endure it.

AEGEUS
                        When death comes, Medea,
It is, for a childless man, utter despair, darkness, extinction. One's
children
Are the life after death.

MEDEA *excited*
                    Do you feel it so? Do you feel it so?
Then—if you had a dog-eyed enemy and needed absolute
    vengeance—you'd kill
The man's children first. Unchild him, ha?
And then unlife him.

146

AEGEUS
          I do not care to think of such horrors.
I have no complete enemy.
     [He stares, and slightly recoils from her.]
                         What is it? What is the matter,
     Medea? You are trembling; wild fever
Flames in your eyes.

MEDEA
          I am well enough . . . . Fools trouble
me, and dogs; but not that—Oh . . ..
[She collapses on the steps and weeps.]

AEGEUS
                         What has happened
     to you?

THE NURSE crouches by her, trying to comfort her.
My dear . . . my love . . .

MEDEA pushes her gently aside, looks up at Aegeus.
               I would not hurt my children. Their father
     hurts them.

AEGEUS
What do you mean, Medea? Jason? What has Jason done?

MEDEA
                                        He has
     betrayed and denied
Both me and them.

AEGEUS
          Jason has done that? Why Why?

                                        147

MEDEA

He has cast
me off and married Creon's young daughter.
And Creon, this very day, is driving us
Into black exile.

AEGEUS

Jason consents to that?

MEDEA

He is glad of it.

AEGEUS

Why—it's
atrocious, it's past belief.

THE NURSE *says in Medea's ear.*
Ask him for refuge! Ask him to receive you in Athens!

MEDEA *stands up, straight and rigid.*
Do you think such men ought to be punished, Aegeus?

AEGEUS
You mean you are driven out into exile?

MEDEA

Into homeless exile.

AEGEUS

Why
that?

MEDEA
Because our presence here is embarrassing

148

To the young bride—Do you not think such men ought
to be punished, Aegeus?

AEGEUS

I think it is villainous.
They told me nothing of this.

MEDEA

Do you not think such men ought
to be punished, Aegeus?

AEGEUS

It's bad.
Where will you go?

MEDEA *solemnly*
If there is any rightness on earth or in heaven,
they will be punished.

AEGEUS

Where
Will you go to, Medea?

MEDEA

What? To death of course.

THE NURSE

Oh . . . She is
all bewildered, sir,
In the deep storm and ocean of grief, or she would ask of you
Refuge in Athens.

MEDEA *in bitter mockery, seeing Aegeus hesitate*
Ah? So I should. That startled the man.—Aegeus:
Will you shelter me in Athens?

149

AEGEUS

                    Why ... yes. Yes ... I will not take
you from Corinth, it would not be right.
I want no trouble with Creon, I am his guest here. If you by your
    own means come to Athens
I will take care of you.

MEDEA

                    I could repay you for it. I know the remedies
        that would make a dry stick
Flame into flower and fruit.

AEGEUS *eagerly*

                    You'd cure my sterility?

MEDEA

                                        I could do so.

AEGEUS
    You are famous for profound knowledge
Of drugs and charms.
        [eagerly]   You'll come to Athens?

MEDEA

                                    If I choose. If the gods
        decide it so. But, Aegeus,
Would you protect me if I came? I have certain enemies.
    If powerful enemies came, baying for my blood,
Would you protect me?

AEGEUS

                    Why ... yes. What enemies? ... Yes.
Athens protects.

    150

MEDEA

        I should need peace and a free mind
While I prepared the medicines to make you well.

AEGEUS

                            You'll have
them, you'll have them, Medea. You've seen the huge stones
In the old sacred war-belt of Athens. Come the four ends of the
    world, they will not break in: you're safe there:
I am your pledge.

MEDEA

            Will you swear it, Aegeus?

AEGEUS

                        Ah? Why?
I promised.

MEDEA

        I trust you: the oath is formal: your cure
Depends on it. You swear by the fruitful earth and high shining
    heaven that you will protect me in Athens
Against all men. Swear it.

AEGEUS

             I swear by the fruitful earth and high
    shining heaven to protect you in Athens
Against all men.

MEDEA

        And if you should break this oath?

AEGEUS

                      I will not
break it.

MEDEA
        If you should break it, the earth
Will give you no bread but death, and the sky no light
But darkness.

AEGEUS *visibly perturbed*
        I will not break it.

MEDEA
                        You must repeat the words,
Aegeus.

AEGEUS
        If I break it, the earth
Will give me no bread but death, and the sky no light
But darkness.

MEDEA
        You have sworn: the gods have heard you.

AEGEUS *uneasily*
                             When will
you come to Athens?

MEDEA
              To . . . Athens? Oh,
To Athens. Why:—if I come, if I live . . . it will be soon.
    The yoke's
On the necks of the horses.—I have some things to do
That men will talk of afterwards with hushed voices: while
    I and my children
Safe in Athens laugh. Is that it? Farewell, Aegeus.
    *[She turns abruptly from him; goes slowly, deep in thought, into
the house.]*

AEGEUS *staring after her*
                                                        May the gods
comfort you, Medea.—To you also farewell,
Ladies of Corinth.

FIRST WOMAN
                    Fair be the gale behind you, sir, and the way
ahead.
[She turns to her companions.]
What is she plotting in her deep mind?
She is juggling with death and life, as a juggler
With a black ball and a white ball.

SECOND WOMAN
No: she is like some distracted city
Sharpening its weapons. Embassies visit her;
The heads of state come to her door;
She receives them darkly.

THE NURSE
                        I beseech you, women,
Not to speak words against my lady whom I love. You know
    what wicked injustice she has to suffer.
[She prays:]
O God, protector of exiles, lord of the holy sky, lead us
To the high rock that Athena loves, and the olive
Garland of Athens.

FIRST WOMAN
                        Athens is beautiful
As a lamp on a rock.
The temples are marble-shafted; light shines and lingers there,
Honey-color among the carved stones
And silver-color on the leaves of the olives.

The maidens are crowned with violets; Athens and Corinth
Are the two crowns of time.

SECOND WOMAN
Mycenae for spears and armor; Sparta
For the stern men and the tall blonde women; and Thebes I
    remember,
Old Thebes and the seven gates in the gray walls—
But rather I praise Athena, the ivory, the golden,
The gray-eyed Virgin, her city.
And also I praise Corinth of the beautiful fountains,
On the fair plain between the two gulfs.

FIRST WOMAN
God-favored cities of the Greek world.
Fortunate those that dwell in them, happy that behold them.

SECOND WOMAN
How can one wish to die? How can that woman
Be drowned in sorrow and bewildered with hatred?

[She does not see Medea, who comes from the door and stands
between the pillars.]

For only to be alive and to see the light
Is beautiful. Only to see the light;
To see a blade of young grass,
Or the gray face of a stone.

FIRST WOMAN   pointing toward Medea
Hush.

MEDEA   proudly and falsely
    As you say. What a marvelous privilege it is
Merely to be alive. And how foolish it would be

154

To spend the one day of life that remains to me—at least
    in Corinth—this tag end of one day
On tears and hatred! Rather I should rejoice, and sing, and give
    gifts; and as to my enemies—
I will be reconciled with them.

FIRST WOMAN *amazed*
                              Reconciled with them!

MEDEA
                                              As you say.
Reconciled. Why should they hate me?
Surely I can appease those people.
They say that gold will buy anything; even friendship, even
    love: at least in Greece,
Among you civilized people, you reasonable and civilized Hellenes.
    —In fact,
We've seen it happen. They bought Jason; Jason's love. Well . . .
I shall buy theirs.
I still have two or three of the treasures that I brought from home,
    things of pure precious gold, which a god
Gave to the kings my ancestors.

[The light darkens, a cloud passing over the sun.]

                              Is it late? It seems to me
That the light darkens.
    [to the Nurse]   Is it evening?

THE NURSE *trembling*
                              No . . . No . . . A cloud.

MEDEA
                                              I hope
    for thunder: let the sky rage: my gifts

155

Will shine the brighter.—Listen, old woman: I want you
To go to Jason and tell him . . . tell him . . . tell him that I am sick
    of hating and weary of evil!
I wish for peace.
I wish to send precious gifts to that pale girl with the yellow hair
Whom he has married: tell him to come and take them—
    and to kiss his boys
Before we go into exile. Tell him to come speedily. Now run, run,
    find him.

THE NURSE
Oh, I'll go. I'll run.
    [tremulously, to chorus]
            Let me pass please.

    [Medea stands looking after her. The Nurse turns back at the limit
    of the scene, and says, wringing her hands.]

But I am terrified. I do not know . . . . . I am terrified. Pray
    to the gods, women, to keep
Evil birds from our hearts!

    [She hurries away. Medea goes into the house.]

Second Act

Medea is sitting on one of the upper
doorsteps. A cloak of woven gold lies across her knee and down the stone
steps. Beside her are two open cases of dark leather. From one she takes
a coronet of golden vine leaves, looks at it and replaces it.

Two serving-women stand in the doorway behind her. The Nurse
stands below her, to one side of the steps. On the other side, at some
distance, the Corinthian women are huddled, like sheep in a storm.

The scene is darker than it was, and the gold cloth shines.

MEDEA

These are the gifts I am sending to the young bride: this golden
    wreath
And this woven-gold veil. They are not without value; there
    is nothing like them in the whole world, or at least
The Western world; the God of the Sun gave them to my father's
    father, and I have kept them
In the deep chest for some high occasion: which has now come.

I have great joy in giving these jewels to Creon's daughter,
    for the glory of life consists in being generous
To one's friends, and . . . merciless to one's enemies . . . you know
    what a friend she has been to me. All Corinth knows.
The slaves talk of it. The old stones in the walls
Have watched and laughed.

*[Medea looks at the gold cloth, and strokes it cautiously with her hand.
It seems to scorch her fingers. Chorus has come nearer to look;
now starts backward.]*

MEDEA

See, it is almost alive. Gold is a living
thing: such pure gold.
But when her body has warmed it, how it will shine!
[to the Nurse]   Why doesn't
he come? What keeps him?

THE NURSE *evidently terrified*

Oh, my lady: presently.
I have but now returned from him. He was beyond the gate,
watching the races—where a monstrous thing
Had happened: a young mare broke from the chariot
And tore with her teeth a stallion.

*[Medea stands up, shakes out the golden cloak, which again smoulders.
She folds it cautiously, lays it in the leather case. The light
has darkened again; she looks anxiously at the clouded sun.]*

MEDEA

He takes his time,
ah? It is intolerable
To sit and wait.
[to the serving-women]
Take these into the house. Keep them at hand
For when I call.

*[They take them in. Medea moves restlessly, under extreme
nervous tension. Speaks to the Nurse.]*
You say that a mare attacked a stallion?

158

THE NURSE
                                          She tore
him cruelly.
I saw him being led away: a black racer: his blood ran down
From the throat to the fetlocks.

MEDEA
                          You're sure he's coming? You're
sure?

THE NURSE
        He said he would.

MEDEA
                    Let him make haste then!

SECOND CORINTHIAN WOMAN
Frightening irrational things
Have happened lately; the face of nature is flawed with omens.

FIRST WOMAN
        Yesterday evening a slave
Came up to the harbor-gate, carrying a basket
Of new-caught fish: one of the fish took fire
And burned in the wet basket with a high flame: the thing
        was witnessed
By many persons.

THIRD WOMAN
                And a black leopard was seen
Gliding through the market-place . . ..

MEDEA *abruptly, approaching the women*
                    You haven't told me yet:
do you not think that Creon's daughter
Will be glad of those gifts?

FIRST WOMAN
                    O Medea, too much wealth
Is sometimes dreadful.

MEDEA
                    She'll be glad, however. She'll take them
and put them on, she'll wear them, she'll strut in them,
She'll peacock in them.—I see him coming now.—The whole
palace will admire her.—Stand away from me, women,
While I make my sick peace.
*[She goes across the scene to meet Jason, but more and more slowly,
and stops. Her attitude indicates her aversion.]*

JASON *entering*
                    Well, I have come. I tell you plainly,
Not for your sake: the children's. Your woman says that you have
your wits again, and are willing
To look beyond your own woes.

[Medea is silent. Jason observes her and says:]
                    It appears doubtful.
—Where are the boys? I have made inquiry: I can find fosterage
for them
In Epidaurus; or any other of several cities
That are Creon's friends. I'll visit them from time to time,
and watch
That they're well kept.

MEDEA *with suppressed violence*
                    You mean . . . take them from me!

160

Be careful, Jason, I am not patient yet.
[*more quietly*]   I am the one who labored
    in pain to bear them, I cannot
Smile while I lose them. But I am learning; I am learning.—
    No, Jason: I will not give up my little ones
To the cold care of strangers. It would be better for them
    to be drowned in the sea than to live with those
Who do not love them, hard faces, harsh hands. It will be far better
    for them to share
My wandering ocean of beggary and bleak exile:—they'll still
    be loved;
And when the sky rages I'll hold them warm
Against my heart. I love them, Jason. Only if you would keep
    them and care for them here in Corinth,
I might consent.

JASON
            Gladly—but they are exiled.

MEDEA
                            —In your own house.

JASON
                    Gladly I'd do it—but you understand
They are exiled, as you are.

MEDEA
                        Innocent; for my rebellion. That's
black.
[*She reaches her hands toward him.*]
        Forgive me, Jason,
As I do you. We have had too much wrath, and our acts
Are closing on us. On me I mean. Retribution is from the gods,
    and it breaks our hearts: but you

Feel no guilt, you fear nothing, nothing can touch you. It is
    wonderful to stand serene above fate
While earthlings wince. If it lasts. It does not always last.—
    Do you love them, Jason?

JASON

                    Ha? Certainly. The children? Certainly!
I am their father.

MEDEA

                    Oh, but that's not enough. If I am to give them
    up to you—be patient with me,
I must question you first. And very deeply; to the quick. If anything
    happend to them,
Would you be grieved?

JASON

                    Nothing will happen to them, Medea,
    if in my care. Rest your mind on it.

MEDEA

You must pardon me: it is not possible to be certain of that.
    If they were . . . killed and their blood
Ran on the floor of the house or down the deep earth—
Would you be grieved?

JASON

                    You have a sick mind. What a weak thing
    a woman is, always dreaming of evil.

MEDEA

Answer me!

162

JASON
     Yes, after I'd cut their killer into red collops—
I'd be grieved.

MEDEA
     That is true: vengeance
Makes grief bearable.—And knowing that . . .. Creon's daughter,
   your wife . . . no doubt will breed
Many other boys.—But, if something should happen to . . . Creon's
   daughter . . ..

JASON
     Enough, Medea. Too much.
Be silent!

MEDEA
     I am to conclude that you love . . . Creon's daughter . . .
More than your sons. They'll have to take the sad journey with
   me.
[to the Nurse]
     Tell the boys to come out
And bid their father farewell.

[The Nurse goes into the house.]

JASON
     I could take them from you
By force, Medea.

MEDEA *violently*
     Try it, you!
[controlling herself]   No, Creon decided otherwise: he said
they will share my exile.—Come, Jason,

163

Let's be friends at last! I know you love them. If they could
stay here in Corinth I'd be content.

JASON

I asked it,
And he refused it.

MEDEA

You asked him to take
My children from me!

[The children come out with their tutor, followed by the Nurse.]

I am quite patient now; I have learned.—
Come, boys: come,
Speak to your father.

[They shrink back.]

No, no, we're friends again. We're not angry
any more.

*[Jason has gone eagerly to meet them on the steps. He drops
to one knee to be more nearly level with them, but they
are shy and reluctant.]*

JASON

Big boys. Tall fellows, ha?
You've grown up since I saw you.

MEDEA

Smile for him, children.
Give him your hands.
*[She turns, and stands rigidly turned away, her face sharp with
pain.]*

THE NURSE *to Jason*
                I think he's afraid of your helmet, sir.

JASON   *to the younger boy*
                                                        What?

What? You'll learn, my man,
Not to fear helmets. The enemy will run from yours
When you grow up to size.
    [to the elder boy]   And you, Captain,
How would you like a horn-tipped bow to hunt rabbits with?
Wolves, I mean.

[He plays with the children. They are less shy of him now.]

FIRST CORINTHIAN WOMAN   *coming close to Medea*
                Don't give them to him,
Medea. If you do it will ache forever.

SECOND WOMAN
                                        You have refuge: take them
    there.
Athens is beautiful . . ..

MEDEA *fiercely*
                Be silent!
Look at him: he loves them—ah? Therefore his dear children
Are not going to that city but a darker city, where no games
    are played, no music is heard.—Do you think
I am a cow lowing after the calf? Or a bitch with pups, licking
The hand that struck her? Watch and see. Watch this man, women:
    he is going to weep. I think
He is going to weep blood, and quite soon, and much more
Than I have wept. Watch and keep silence.
    [She goes toward the group on the steps.] Jason,

                                                        165

Are the boys dear to you? I think I am satisfied that you love
    them . . ..
    [She weeps, covering her face.]
        Oh, Oh, Oh . . ..

*[Jason stands up and turns to her, one of the boys clinging to each
of his hands. He has made friends with them.]*

JASON
These two young heroes . . . God's hand, Medea, what is it?
What is the matter?

MEDEA *makes with both hands a gesture of pushing down
something, and flings her head back proudly.*
            Nothing. It is hard to let them go.
Are they very sweet to you? You love them dearly?—This I have
    thought of:
You shall take them to . . . Creon's daughter, your wife . . .
    and make them kneel to her, and ask her
To ask her father to let them stay here in Corinth. He'll grant
    it, he is growing old, he denies her nothing.
Even that hard king loves his only child.
What she asks is done.—You will go with the boys, Jason, and speak
    for them,—they are not skillful yet
In supplication—and I'll send gifts. I'll put gifts in their hands.
    People say that gifts
Will persuade even the gods.—Is it well thought of?
Will she listen to us?

JASON
            Why, if I ask it! She'd hardly refuse
    me anything. And I believe that you're right,
She can rule Creon.

MEDEA *to the Nurse*
                    Bring me those gold things.
[*to the children*]   Dear ones, brave
little falcons . . . little pawns of my agony . . .
Go ask that proud breastless girl of her bitter charity
Whether she will let you nest here until your wings fledge, while
    far your mother
Flies the dark storm . . . .
[*She weeps again.*]

JASON
                    I'm sorry for you. Parting is hard.

MEDEA
                                                I can
    bear it.
And worse too.

[*The Nurse and a serving-woman bring the gifts.*]

                    Oh, here: here are the things: take them, darlings,
Into your little hands.
[*giving them to the children*]
                    Hold carefully by the cases: don't touch
    the gold,
Or it might . . . tarnish.

JASON
                    Why! These are king's treasures.
You shouldn't, Medea: it's too much. Creon's house
Has gold enough of its own.

MEDEA
                    Oh—if she'll wear them. What should
    I want

With woven golden vanities?—Black is my wear. The woman
    ought to be very happy
With such jewels—and such a husband—ah? Her sun is rising,
    mine going down—I hope
To a red sunset.—The little gold wreath is pretty, isn't it?

JASON   *doubtfully*

                                            It looks
like fire . . ..

MEDEA
                 Vine leaves: the flashing
Arrow-sharp leaves. They have weight, though.
*[She takes the cases from the children, gives them to the Nurse
and the Tutor.]*   Gold is too heavy
a burden for little hands. Carry them, you,
Until you come to the palace.—Farewell, sweet boys: brave little
    trudging pilgrims from the black wave
To the white desert: take the stuff in, be sure you lay it in her
    own hands.
Come back and tell me what happens.
[She turns abruptly away from them.]
                           Tell me what happens.

*[The children go out reluctantly, Jason holding their hands. The Nurse
and the Tutor have gone ahead. Medea hides her face, weeping;
then lifts her head proudly, and walks toward chorus.]*
Rejoice, women. The gifts are given; the bait is laid.
The gods roll their great eyes over Creon's house and quietly
    smile: for no rat nor cony
Would creep into the open undisguised traps
That take the proud race of man. They snap at a shiny bait; they'll
    believe anything. I too
Have been fooled in my time: now I shall triumph. That robe
    of bright-flowing gold, that bride-veil, that fish-net

168

To catch a young slender salmon—not mute, she'll sing:
  her delicate body writhes in the meshes,
The golden wreath binds her bright head with light: she'll dance,
  she'll sing loudly:
Would I were there to hear it, that proud one howling.—Look,
  the sun's out again, the clouds are gone,
All's gay and clear. I wish the deep earth would open and swallow
  us—
Before I do what comes next.
I wish all life would perish, and the holy gods in high heaven
  die, before my little ones
Come home to my hands.

FIRST CORINTHIAN WOMAN
It would be better for you, Medea, if the earth
Opened her jaws and took you down into darkness.
But one thing you will not do, for you cannot,
You will not hurt your own children, though wrath like
  plague-boils
Aches, your mind in a fire-haze
Bites the purple apples of pain—no blood-lapping
Beast of the field, she-bear nor lioness,
Nor the lean wolf-bitch,
Hurts her own tender whelps; nor the yellow-eyed,
Scythe-beaked and storm-shouldered
Eagle that tears the lambs has ever made prey
Of the fruit of her own tree—

MEDEA
                                How could that girl's death slake
me?

THIRD WOMAN *coming forward from the others*
  I am sick with terror.
I'll run to the palace, I'll warn them.

MEDEA

Will you?—Go. Go, if you will.
God and my vengeful goddess are doing these things: you cannot
    prevent them, but you could easily fall
In the same fire.

THIRD WOMAN   *retreating*
        I am afraid to go.

MEDEA

You are wise. Anyone
Running between me and my justice will reap
What no man wants.

FIRST WOMAN
        Not justice: vengeance.
You have suffered evil, you wish to inflict evil.

MEDEA
I do according to nature what I have to do.

FIRST WOMAN
I have heard evil
Answering evil as thunder answers the lightning,
A great waste voice in the hollow sky,
And all that they say is death. I have heard vengeance
Like an echo under a hill answering vengeance,
Great hollow voices: all that they say is death.

SECOND WOMAN

The sword speaks
And the spear answers: the city is desolate.
The nations remember old wrongs and destroy each other,
And no man binds up their wounds.

170

FIRST WOMAN
                                But justice
Builds a firm house.

MEDEA
                    The doors of her house are vengeance.

SECOND WOMAN
                                                    I
    dreamed that someone
Gave good for evil, and the world was amazed.

MEDEA
Only a coward or a madman gives good for evil.—Did you hear
    a thin music
Like a girl screaming? Or did I perhaps imagine it? Hark,
    it is music.

THIRD WOMAN
Let me go, Medea!
I'll be mute, I'll speak to no one. I cannot bear—
Let me go to my house!

MEDEA
                        You will stay here,
And watch the end.

    [The women are beginning to mill like scared cattle, huddled
    and circular.]

                        You will be quiet, you women. You came
    to see
How the barbarian woman endures betrayal: watch and you'll
    know.

                                                171

SECOND WOMAN
My heart is a shaken cup
Of terror: the thin black wine
Spills over all my flesh down to my feet.

FIRST WOMAN
She fled from her father's house in a storm of blood,
In a blood-storm she flew up from Thessaly,
Now here and dark over Corinth she widens
Wings to ride up the twisted whirlwind
And talons to hold with—
Let me flee this dark place and the pillared doorway.

SECOND WOMAN
I hear the man-wolf on the snow hill
Howl to the soaring moon—

THIRD WOMAN
The demon comes in through the locked door
And strangles the child—

SECOND WOMAN
Blood is the seed of blood, hundredfold the harvest,
The gleaners that follow it, their feet are crimson—

FIRST WOMAN
I see the whirlwind hanging from the black sky
Like a twisted rope,
Like an erect serpent, its tail tears the earth,
It is braided of dust and lightning,
Who will fly in it? Let me hide myself
From these night-shoring pillars and the dark door.

172

MEDEA

Have patience,
women. Be quiet.
I am quite sure something has happened; presently someone
Will bring us news.

THIRD WOMAN

Look! The children are coming.

SECOND WOMAN
They have bright things in their hands: their faces are clear
and joyous: was all that fear
A dream, a dream?

[The Tutor enters with the children. The elder child carries
a decorated bow and arrows; the younger has a doll, a brightly
painted wooden warrior. Medea, gazing at the children, retreats
slowly backward from them.]

THE TUTOR

Rejoice, Medea, I bring good news.
The princess graciously
Received your presents and smiled: it is peace between you. She
has welcomed the little boys, they are safe from exile.
They'll be kept here. Their father is joyful.

MEDEA *coldly, her hands clenched in the effort of self-control*

Yes?

THE TUTOR
All Creon's house is well pleased. When we first went in
The serving-women came and fondled the children; it was rumored
through all the household that you and Jason

Were at peace again: like word of a victory
Running through a wide city, when people gather in the streets
    to be glad together: and we brought the boys
Into the hall; we put those costly gifts in their hands; then Jason
Led them before the princess. At first she looked angrily at them
    and turned away, but Jason said,
"Don't be angry at your friends. You ought to love
Those whom I love. Look what they've brought you, dear,"
    and she looked and saw
In the dark boxes the brilliant gold: she smiled then,
And marveled at it. Afterward she caressed the children; she even
    said that this little one's
Hair was like fine-spun gold. Then Jason gave them these toys
    and we came away.

MEDEA

                              Yes.—if this
Were all. If this were all, old man—
I'd have your bony loins beaten to a blood-froth
For the good news you bring.

THE TUTOR

                              My lady—!

MEDEA

                                        There's more, however.
It will soon come.
[*She moves restlessly in the direction they have come from; stands
gazing; returns toward the doorsteps. The children shyly approach
her and show their toys. She, with violent self-constraint, looks
at them; but folds her hands in her cloak, not to touch them.*]

THE ELDER CHILD *drawing the little bow*
              Look, Mother.

174

MEDEA *suddenly weeping*
                              Take them away from me!
I cannot bear. I cannot bear.
[*She sits on the steps, and draws the cloak over her face.*]

THE TUTOR
                              Children, come quickly.
[*He shepherds them up the steps and disappears in the house;
but they turn back and stand in the doorway.*]

FIRST WOMAN
If there is any mercy or forbearance in heaven
Let it reach down and touch that dark mind
To save it from what it dreams—

      [*A young slave dashes in, panting and distraught. He has run from
      Creon's house.*]

THE SLAVE
                              Where is Medea?

SECOND WOMAN
                                        What
      has happened? What horror drives you?
Are spears hunting behind you?

      THE SLAVE *He sees Medea, still sitting on the steps, her face
      and head hidden.*   Flee for your life, Medea!
      I am Jason's man, but you were good to me
While I was here in the house. Can you hear me? Escape, Medea!

MEDEA *slowly, drawing the cloak slowly from her head, and still
sitting*
I hear you. Draw breath; say quietly

What you have seen. It must have been something notable,
   the way your eyes
Bulge in the whites.

   THE SLAVE
                        If you have horses, Medea, drive! Or a boat
      on the shore,
Sail!

   MEDEA
   But first you must tell me about that beautiful girl who was
   lately married: your great man's daughter:
Are they all quite well?

   THE SLAVE
                        My ears ring with the crying, my eyes
      are scalded. She put on the gold garments—
Did you do it, Medea?

   MEDEA
                        I did it. Speak quietly.

   THE SLAVE
                                    You are avenged.
You are horribly avenged. It is too much.
The gods will hate you.

   MEDEA   *avid, but still sitting*
                        That is my care. Did anyone die with her?

   THE SLAVE
   Creon!

MEDEA *solemnly, standing up*
          Where is pride now?
Tell me all that you saw. Speak slowly.

THE SLAVE
                                        He tried to save her—he
died! Corinth is masterless.
All's in amazed confusion, and some are looting, but they'll
avenge him—
     [*He hears someone coming behind him.*]
                    I'm going on!
Someone is going to die.
     [*He runs to the far side of the scene, and exits while Medea speaks.
     Meanwhile the light has been changing, and soon the sun will set.*]

MEDEA
                    Here comes a more stable witness.

[*The Nurse enters.*]

                                                      Old
     friend:
Catch your breath; take your time. I want the whole tale, every
     gesture and cry. I have labored for this.

THE NURSE
Death is turned loose! I've hobbled and run, and fallen—

MEDEA
                                                Please,
     Nurse: I am very happy: go slowly.
Tell me these things in order from the beginning.

177

As when you used to dress me, when I was little, in my father's
    house: you used to say
"One thing at a time; one thing and then the next."

[The light has changed to a flare of sunset.]

THE NURSE

                                     My eyes
    are blistered,
My throat's like a dry straw . . . . There was a long mirror
    on the wall, and when her eyes saw it—
After the children had gone with Jason—she put her hands
    in the cases and took those gold things—and I
Watched, for I feared something might happen to her, but I never
    thought
So horribly—she placed on her little head the bright golden
    wreath, she gathered the flowing gold robe
Around her white shoulders,
And slender flanks,
And gazed at the golden girl in the metal mirror, going back
    and forth
On tiptoe almost; and swung her leg from the hip, to see the
    flexible gold
Moulding the thigh. But suddenly horror began. I . . . Oh, Oh. . . .

MEDEA
    You are not suffering.
You saw it, you did not feel it. Speak plainly.

THE NURSE

                              Her face went white;
She staggered a few steps, bending over, and fell
Into the great throne-chair; then a serving-woman
Began to call for water thinking she had fainted, but saw the foam

178

Start on her lips, and the eyes rolling, and screamed instead. Then
    some of them
Ran after Jason, others ran to fetch Creon: and that doomed girl
Frightfully crying started up from the chair; she ran, she was like
    a torch, and the gold crown
Like a comet streamed fire; she tore at it but it clung to her head;
    the golden cloak
Was white-hot, flaying the flesh from the living bones; blood
    mixed with fire ran down, she fell, she burned
On the floor, writhing. Then Creon came and flung himself
    on her, hoping to choke
That rage of flame, but it ran through him, his own agony
Made him forget his daughter's. The fire stuck to the flesh,
    it glued him to her; he tried to stand up,
He tore her body and his own. The burnt flesh broke
In lumps from the bones.
    [She covers her eyes with her hands.]
                        I have finished. They lie there.
Eyeless, disfaced, untouchable; middens of smoking flesh laced
    with molten gold . . ..
    [nearly a scream]   No! I have finished.
I have no more.

        MEDEA
                I want all.
Had they died when you came away?

        THE NURSE
                                I am not able . . . have
    mercy . . .. No, the harsh tides of breath
Still whistled in the black mouths. No one could touch them.
    Jason stood in their smoke, and his hands tore
His unhelmeted hair.

You have told good news well: I'll
reward you.
As for those people, they will soon die. Their woes are over
too soon. Mine are not.
Jason's are not.

*[She turns abruptly from her, toward the children who have
been standing by the doorway, fascinated, not comprehending
but watching.]*

My little falcons!—Listen to me: laugh and be
glad: we have accomplished it.
Our enemies were great and powerful, they were full of cold
pride, they ruled all this country—they are down
in the ashes.
Crying like dogs, cowering in the ashes, in their own ashes. They
went down with the sun, and the sun will rise
And not see them again. He will think "Perhaps they are sleeping,
they feasted late,
At noon they will walk in the garden." Oh, no, oh, no!
They will not walk in the garden. No one has ever injured
me but suffered more
Than I had suffered.

[She turns from the children.]

Therefore this final sacrifice I intended glares
in my eyes
Like a lion on a ridge.

[turning back to the children]

We still hate, you know:—a person nearer
than these, more vile, more contemptible,
Whom I . . . I cannot. If he were my own hands I would
cut him off, or my eyes, I would gouge him out—
But not you: that was madness.

[She turns from them.]   So Jason will be able to say, "I have
lost much,
But not all: I have children: my sons are well." That
too is unbearable.

[She stands staring, agonized, one hand picking at the other.]
                    I want him crushed, boneless, crawling . . .
I have no choice.
   [resolutely, to chorus]
                 You there! You thought me soft and submissive
like a common woman—who takes a blow
And cries a little, and she wipes her face
And runs about the housework, loving her master? I am not such
a woman.

FIRST WOMAN
               Awake, Medea!
Awake from the evil dream. Catch up your children and flee.
Farther than Athens, farther than Thrace or Spain, flee
   to the world's end.
Fire and death have done your bidding,
Are you not fed full with evil?
Is it not enough?

MEDEA
               No. Loathing is endless.
Hate is a bottomless cup, I will pour and pour.
   [She turns fiercely to the children.]   Children—
   [suddenly melting]   . . . O
   my little ones!
What was I dreaming?—My babes, my own!
   [She kneels to them, taking their hands.]   Never, never, never,
   never
Shall my own babes be hurt. Not if every war-hound
   and spearslave in headless Corinth
Were on the track.
   [still kneeling, to chorus]
              Look, their sweet lips are trembling: look,
   women, the little mouths: I frightened them

With those wild words: they stood and faced me, they never
flinched.
Look at their proud young eyes! My eaglets, my golden ones!
[She kisses them, then holds them off and gazes at them.]   O
sweet small faces . . . like the pale wild-roses
That bloom where the cliff breaks toward the brilliant sea: the
delicate form and color, the dear, dear fragrance
Of your sweet breath . . ..
[She continues gazing at them; her face changes.]

THE NURSE
                              My lady, make haste, haste!
Take them and flee. Flee away from here! Someone will come
soon.

[Medea still gazes at the children. The Nurse clutches her shoulder.]
Oh—listen to me.
Spears will come, death will come. All Corinth is in confusion
and headless anarchy, unkinged and amazed
Around that horror you made: therefore they linger:
yet in a moment
Its avengers come!

*[Medea looks up from staring at the children. Her face has changed;
the love has gone out of it. She speaks in a colorless tired voice.]*

MEDEA
                              I have a sword in the house.
I can defend you.
*[She stands up stiffly and takes the children by their shoulders;
holds the elder one in front of her, toward chorus; speaks with
cold intensity.]*
                              Would you say that this child
Has Jason's eyes?

[The women are silent, in terror gazing at her.]
182

. . . They are his cubs. They have his blood.
As long as they live I shall be mixed with him.
[She looks down at the children, speaks tenderly but hopelessly.]
                                                    Children:
It is evening. See, evening has come. Come, little ones,
Into the house. Evening brings all things home. It brings the bird
    to the bough and the lamb to the fold—
And the child to the mother. We must not think too much:
    people go mad
If they think too much.
*[She has pushed the children gently into the house. In the doorway,
behind them, she flings up her hands as if to tear her hair
out by the roots; then quietly goes in. The great door closes; the iron
noise of the bolt is driven home.]*

THE NURSE
                            No! No!
*[She rushes toward the door, but sinks down on the steps, helpless,
her hand reaching up and beating feebly against the foot
of the door.]*   No . . .

FIRST WOMAN
What has happened?

SECOND WOMAN
That crown of horrors . . ..

*[They speak like somnambulists, and stand frozen. There is a moment
of silence.]*

CHILD'S VOICE   *in the house, shrill, broken off*
Mother Ai—!

*[The women press toward the door, crying more or less
simultaneously:]*

                                                        183

Medea, no!
Prevent her! Save them!
Open the door—
[They listen for an answer.]

ELDER CHILD'S VOICE
You've hurt him! The blood. The blood. Oh, Mother!

THIRD WOMAN *below the steps, farthest from the door*
A god is here, Medea, he calls to you, he forbids you—

[The Nurse has risen, and beats feebly on the door, stooping and bent over. First Woman stands beside her very erect, with her back against the door, covering her ears with her hands. They are silent.]

ELDER CHILD'S VOICE *clear, but as if hypnotized*
She is hunting me . . ..
She is hunting me . . .. She is hunting . . .. Aah!

[Lamentation—keening—is heard in the house. It rises and falls, and continues to the end, but often nearly inaudible. It is now twilight.]

THE NURSE *limps down the steps and says*
There is no hope in heaven or earth. It is done.
It was destined when she was born, now it is done.
[wailing]   Oh, Oh, Oh.

THIRD WOMAN *with terror, looking into the shadows*
Who is coming?
Someone is running at us!

FIRST WOMAN *quietly*
                                    The accursed man.
Jason.

SECOND WOMAN
    He has a sword!

FIRST WOMAN
                    I am more afraid of the clinging contagion
of his misfortunes.
A man the gods are destroying.

    JASON *enters rapidly, disheveled and shaking, a drawn sword
    in his hand.*   Where is that murderess? Here
    in the house?
Or has she fled? She'll have to hide in the heavy metal darkness
    and caves of the earth—and there
I'll crawl and find her.

    [No answer. The women draw away from him as he moves toward
    the door. He stops and turns on them, drawing his left hand across
    his face, as if his eyes were bewildered.]
                    Are you struck dumb? Are you shielding
    her?
Where is Medea?

FIRST WOMAN
                You caused these things. She was faithful
    to you and you broke faith.
Horror is here.

    JASON
                Uncaused. There was no reason . . . .. Tell me at least
Whether she took my boys with her? Creon's people would kill
    them for what she has done: I'd rather save them
Than punish her. Help me in this.

THE NURSE *wailing*
                        Oh. Oh, Oh . . .

                                                185

JASON *looking sharply at the nurse*

So she has killed
herself.
Good. She never lacked courage . . . . I'll take my sons away
to the far end of the earth, and never
Speak of these things again.

THE NURSE *wailing*

Oh, Oh, Oh . . . .

[Lamentation from the house answers.]

JASON *with a queer slyness, for he is trying to cheat himself
out of believing what he dreads. He glances at the door, furtively,
over his shoulder.*   Is she lying in there?
Honorable at least in her death.—I might have known it.

[They remain silent.]   Well,
answer!

FIRST WOMAN *pointing toward Creon's house*
Death is there; death is here.
But you are both blind and deaf: how can I tell you?

JASON *is silent, then says slowly*

But . . . the
. . . children are well?

FIRST WOMAN

I do not know
Whether Medea lives or is dead.

JASON *stares at her; turns suddenly to the door and hammers
on it with his sword-hilt.*   Open! Open! Open!

186

[He flings down the sword and sets his shoulder against the door;
pushes in vain; returns halfway down the steps, and says pitiably]
                                                  Women,

          I am alone. Help me.
Help me to break the bolt.

SECOND WOMAN
                    Our shoulders?

JASON
                              Go and find help . . ..

[The door opens behind him. It is now fairly dark; the interior
of the house is lighted. Two serving-women come from behind
the door-jambs, and place two flickering lamps just outside
the door, at the bases of the pillars, and withdraw themselves.
They move symmetrically, like mirror-images of each other,
one right-handed, one left-handed. Chorus draws back in fear;
Jason stands on the steps, bewildered. Medea comes into the
doorway; her hand and clothing are bloodmarked.]

MEDEA
What feeble night-bird overcome by misfortunes beats at my door?
     Can this be that great adventurer,
The famous lord of the seas and delight of women, the heir of rich
     Corinth—this crying drunkard
On the dark doorstep?—Yet you've not had enough. You have
     come to drink the last bitter drops.
I'll pour them for you.

JASON
                    What's that stain on your hand?

MEDEA

The wine
I was pouring for you spilled on my hand.
Dear were the little grapes that were crushed to make it; dear
were the vineyards.

JASON

I came to kill you, Medea,
Like a caught beast, like a crawling viper. Give me my sons, that
I may save them from Creon's men,
I'll go quietly away.

MEDEA

Hush, they are sleeping. Perhaps I will
let you look at them: you cannot have them.
But the hour is late, you ought to go home to that high-born
bride; the night has fallen, surely she longs for you.
Surely her flesh is not crusted black, nor her mouth a horror.

[Jason kneels on the steps, painfully groping for his sword.]

She
is very young,
But surely she will be fruitful.—Your sword you want?
There it is. Not that step, the next lower. No, the next higher.

JASON *finds it and stands erect.*
I'll kill you first and then find my sons.

MEDEA

You must be careful, Jason.
Do you see the two fire-snakes
That guard this door?
[indicating the two lamps]

Here and here: one on each side:
two serpents. Their throats are swollen with poison,
Their eyes are burning coals and their tongues are fire. They
    are coiled ready to strike: if you come near them,
They'll make you what Creon is. But stand there very quietly,
    I'll let you
Look at your sons.
[She speaks to someone in the house, behind the left door-jamb.]
                Bring them across the doorway that
he may see them.
*[She stands back, and two serving-women pass within the doorway
from left to right, bearing the slain children on a litter between
them. It stands a moment in the gape of the door, and passes.]*

JASON   *dropping the sword, flinging his hands to his temples*
                I knew it already.
I knew it before I saw it. No wild beast could have done it.

MEDEA
                                                    I have
    done it: because I loathed you more
Than I loved them. Mine is the triumph.

JASON
                        Your triumph.
No iron-fleshed demon of those whom your father worships
In that blood-crusted temple—Did you feel nothing, no pity,
    are you pure evil? I should have killed you
The day I saw you.

MEDEA
                I tore my own heart and laughed: I was tearing
yours.

JASON
      Will you laugh while I strangle you?

MEDEA
I would still laugh.—Beware my door-holders, Jason! these eager
      serpents.—I'd still be joyful
To know that every bone of your life is broken; you are left
      hopeless, friendless, mateless, childless,
Avoided by gods and men, unclean with awful excess of grief—
      childless—

JASON *exhausted*
            It is no matter now
Who lives, or who dies.

MEDEA
                  Go down to your ship Argo and weep
      beside it, that rotting hulk on the harbor-beach
Drawn dry astrand, never to be launched again—even the weeds
      and barnacles on the warped keel
Are dead and stink:—that's your last companion—
And only hope: for some time one of the rotting timbers
Will fall on your head and kill you—meanwhile sit there
      and mourn, remembering the infinite evil, and the good
That has turned evil.

JASON
            Exult in evil, gloat your fill, have your glory.

MEDEA
My heart's blood bought it.

JASON
                  Enjoy it then.

190

Only give me my boys: the little pitiful violated bodies: that
    I may bury them
In some kind place.

MEDEA
                To you?—You would betray even the little
    bodies: coin them for silver,
Sell them for power. No.

JASON *kneeling*
                    Let me touch their dear flesh, let me
    touch their hair!

MEDEA
                No. They are mine.
They are going with me: the chariot is in the gate. You had love
    and betrayed it; now of all men
You are utterly the most miserable. As I of women.
    But I, a woman, a foreigner, alone
Against you and the might of Corinth—have met you throat
    for throat, evil for evil. Now I go forth
Under the cold eyes of the weakness-despising stars:—not me they
    scorn.

*[She goes out of sight behind the right door-jamb, following the dead
children. Jason stumbles up the steps to follow her, and falls
between the two flickering lamps. The door remains open, the light
in the house is partially extinguished. A music of mixed triumph
and lamentation is heard to pass from the house, and diminish into
the distance beyond it.]*

New Directions Paperbooks—A Partial Listing

Walter Abish, *How German Is It.* NDP508.
Ahmed Ali, *Twilight in Delhi.* NDP782.
John Allman, *Scenarios for a Mixed Landscape.* NDP619.
Alfred Andersch, *Efraim's Book.* NDP779.
Sherwood Anderson, *Poor White.* NDP763.
Wayne Andrews, *The Surrealist Parade.* NDP689.
David Antin, *Tuning.* NDP570.
G. Apollinaire, *Selected Writings.*† NDP310.
Jimmy S. Baca, *Martin & Meditations.* NDP648.
Balzac, *Colonel Chabert.* NDP848.
Djuna Barnes, *Nightwood.* NDP98.
J. Barzun, *An Essay on French Verse.* NDP708.
H. E. Bates, *A Month by the Lake.* NDP669.
A Party for the Girls. NDP653.
Charles Baudelaire, *Flowers of Evil.* †NDP684.
Paris Spleen. NDP294.
Bei Dao, *Old Snow.* NDP727.
Gottfried Benn, *Primal Vision.* NDP322.
Adolfo Bioy Casares, *A Russian Doll.* NDP745.
Carmel Bird, *The Bluebird Café.* NDP707.
Johannes Bobrowski, *Shadow Lands.* NDP788.
Wolfgang Borchert, *The Man Outside.* NDP319.
Jorge Luis Borges, *Labyrinths.* NDP186.
Seven Nights. NDP576.
Kay Boyle, *The Crazy Hunter.* NDP770.
Fifty Stories. NDP741.
Kamau Brathwaite, *MiddlePassages.* NDP776.
Black + Blues. NDP815.
William Bronk, *Selected Poems.* NDP816.
M. Bulgakov, *Flight & Bliss.* NDP593.
The Life of M. de Moliere. NDP601.
Frederick Busch, *Absent Friends.* NDP721.
Veza Canetti, *Yellow Street.* NDP709.
Anne Carson, *Glass, Irony & God.* NDP808.
Joyce Cary, *Mister Johnson.* NDP631.
Hayden Carruth, *Tell Me Again.* . . . NDP677.
Camilo José Cela, *Mazurka for Two Dead Men.* NDP789.
Louis-Ferdinand Céline,
Death on the Installment Plan. NDP330.
Journey to the End of the Night. NDP542.
René Char, *Selected Poems.* †NDP734.
Jean Cocteau, *The Holy Terrors.* NDP212.
M. Collis, *She Was a Queen.* NDP716.
Gregory Corso, *Long Live Man.* NDP127.
Herald of the Autochthonic Spirit. NDP522.
Robert Creeley, *Windows.* NDP687.
Guy Davenport, *7 Greeks.* NDP799.
Margaret Dawe, *Nissequott.* NDP775.
Osamu Dazai, *The Setting Sun.* NDP258.
No Longer Human. NDP357.
Mme. de Lafayette, *The Princess of Cleves.* NDP660.
Debra DiBlasi, *Drought.* NDP836.
Robert Duncan, *Selected Poems.* NDP754.
Wm. Empson, *7 Types of Ambiguity.* NDP204.
S. Endo, *Deep River.* NDP820.
The Samurai. NDP839.
Caradoc Evans, *Nothing to Pay.* NDP800.
Wm. Everson, *The Residual Years.* NDP263.
Lawrence Ferlinghetti, *A Coney Island of the Mind.* NDP74.
These Are My Rivers. NDP786.
Ronald Firbank, *Five Novels.* NDP581.
F. Scott Fitzgerald, *The Crack-up.* NDP757.
Gustave Flaubert, *A Simple Heart.* NDP819.
J. Gahagan, *Did Gustav Mahler Ski?* NDP711.
Forrest Gander, *Science & Steepleflower.* NDP861.
Gandhi, *Gandi on Non-Violence.* NDP197.
Gary, Romain, *Promise at Dawn.* NDP635.
W. Gerhardie, *Futility.* NDP722.
Goethe, *Faust,* Part I. NDP70.
Allen Grossman, *Philosopher's Window.* NDP807.
Martin Grzimek, *Shadowlife.* NDP705.
Guigonnat, Henri, *Daemon in Lithuania.* NDP592.
Lars Gustafsson, *The Death of a Beekeeper.* NDP523.
A Tiler's Afternoon. NDP761.
Knut Hamsun, *Dreamers.* NDP821.

John Hawkes, *The Beetle Leg.* NDP239.
Second Skin. NDP146.
H. D. *Collected Poems.* NDP611.
Helen in Egypt. NDP380.
Selected Poems. NDP658.
Tribute to Freud. NDP572.
Trilogy. NDP866.
Herman Hesse, *Siddhartha.* NDP65.
Susan Howe, *The Nonconformist's Memorial.* NDP755.
Vicente Huidobro, *Selected Poetry.* NDP520.
C. Isherwood, *All the Conspirators.* NDP480.
The Berlin Stories. NDP134.
Lêdo Ivo, *Snake's Nest.* NDP521.
Fleur Jaeggy, *Last Vanities.* NDP856.
Henry James, *The Sacred Fount.* NDP790.
Gustav Janouch, *Conversations with Kafka.* NDP313.
Alfred Jarry, *Ubu Roi.* NDP105.
Robinson Jeffers, *Cawdor and Medea.* NDP293.
B. S. Johnson, *Christie Malry's.* . . NDP600.
G. Josipovici, *In a Hotel Garden.* NDP801.
James Joyce, *Stephen Hero.* NDP133.
Franz Kafka, *Amerika.* NDP117.
Mary Karr, *The Devil's Tour.* NDP768.
Bob Kaufman, *The Ancient Rain.* NDP514.
John Keene, *Annotations.* NDP809.
H. von Kleist, *Prince Friedrich.* NDP462.
Dezsö Kosztolányi, *Anna Edes.* NDP772.
Rüdiger Kremer, *The Color of Snow.* NDP743.
M. Krleža, *On the Edge of Reason.* NDP810.
Jules Laforgue, *Moral Tales.* NDP594.
P. Lal, *Great Sanskrit Plays.* NDP142.
Tommaso Landolfi, *Gogol's Wife.* NDP155.
D. Larsen, *Stitching Porcelain.* NDP710.
James Laughlin, *The Secret Room.* NDP837.
Lautréamont, *Maldoror.* NDP207.
D. H. Lawrence, *Quetzalcoatl.* NDP864.
Siegfried Lenz, *The German Lesson.* NDP618.
Denise Levertov, *Breathing the Water.* NDP640.
Collected Earlier Poems 1940–60. NDP475.
The Life Around Us. NDP843.
Poems 1960–1967. NDP549.
Poems 1968–1972. NDP629.
Sands of the Well. NDP849.
The Stream and the Sapphire. NDP844.
Harry Levin, *James Joyce.* NDP87.
Li Ch'ing-chao, *Complete Poems.* NDP492.
Li Po, *Selected Poems.* NDP823.
C. Lispector, *Soulstorm.* NDP671.
The Hour of the Star. NDP733.
Selected Crónicas. NDP834.
Garciá Lorca, *Five Plays.* NDP232.
Selected Poems. †NDP114.
Three Tragedies. NDP52.
Michael McClure, *Simple Eyes.* NDP780.
Carson McCullers, *The Member of the Wedding.* (Playscript) NDP153.
X. de Maistre, *Voyage Around My Room.* NDP791.
Stéphane Mallarmé,† *Selected Poetry and Prose.* NDP529.
Bernadette Mayer, *A Bernadette Mayer Reader.* NDP739.
Thomas Merton, *Asian Journal.* NDP394.
New Seeds of Contemplation. NDP337.
Selected Poems. NDP85.
Thoughts on the East. NDP802.
The Way of Chuang Tzu. NDP276.
Zen and the Birds of Appetite. NDP261.
Henri Michaux, *A Barbarian in Asia.* NDP622.
Selected Writings. NDP264.
Henry Miller, *The Air-Conditioned Nightmare.* NDP302.
Aller Retour New York. NDP753.
Big Sur & The Oranges. NDP161.
The Colossus of Maroussi. NDP75.
A Devil in Paradise. NDP765.
Into the Heart of Life. NDP728.
The Smile at the Foot of the Ladder. NDP386.
Y. Mishima, *Confessions of a Mask.* NDP253.
Death in Midsummer. NDP215.
Frédéric Mistral, *The Memoirs.* NDP632.

For a complete listing request free catalog from
New Directions, 80 Eighth Avenue, New York 10011   †Bilingual

Eugenio Montale, *It Depends.*† NDP507.
Selected Poems.† NDP193.
Paul Morand, *Fancy Goods/Open All Night.* NDP567.
Vladimir Nabokov, *Nikolai Gogol.* NDP78.
Laughter in the Dark. NDP729.
The Real Life of Sebastian Knight. NDP432.
P. Neruda, *The Captain's Verses.*† NDP345.
Residence on Earth.† NDP340.
Fully Empowered. NDP792.
New Directions in Prose & Poetry (Anthology).
Available from #17 forward to #55.
Robert Nichols, *Arrival.* NDP437.
J. F. Nims, *The Six-Cornered Snowflake.* NDP700.
Charles Olson, *Selected Writings.* NDP231.
Toby Olson, *The Life of Jesus.* NDP417.
George Oppen, *Collected Poems.* NDP418.
István Örkeny, *The Flower Show/*
The Toth Family. NDP536.
Wilfred Owen, *Collected Poems.* NDP210.
José Emilio Pacheco, *Battles in the Desert.* NDP637.
Selected Poems.† NDP638.
Michael Palmer, *At Passages.* NDP803.
Nicanor Parra, *Antipoems: New & Selected.* NDP603.
Boris Pasternak, *Safe Conduct.* NDP77.
Kenneth Patchen, *Because It Is.* NDP83.
Collected Poems. NDP284.
Selected Poems. NDP160.
Ota Pavel, *How I Came to Know Fish.* NDP713.
Octavio Paz, *Collected Poems.* NDP719.
A Draft of Shadows.† NDP489.
Selected Poems. NDP574.
Sunstone.† NDP735.
A Tale of Two Gardens. NDP841.
A Tree Within.† NDP661.
Victor Pelevin, *The Yellow Arrow;* NDP845.
Omon Ra. NDP851.
Ezra Pound, *ABC of Reading.* NDP89.
The Cantos. NDP824.
Confucius. NDP285.
Confucius to Cummings. (Anth.) NDP126.
Diptych Rome-London. NDP783.
Guide to Kulchur. NDP257.
Literary Essays. NDP250.
Personae. NDP697.
Selected Cantos. NDP304.
Selected Poems. NDP66.
Caradog Prichard, *One Moonlit Night.* NDP835.
Eça de Queirós, *Ilustrious House of Ramires.* NDP785.
Raymond Queneau, *The Blue Flowers.* NDP595.
Exercises in Style. NDP513.
Mary de Rachewiltz, *Ezra Pound.* NDP405.
Raja Rao, *Kanthapura.* NDP224.
Herbert Read, *The Green Child.* NDP208.
P. Reverdy, *Selected Poems.*† NDP346.
Kenneth Rexroth, *An Autobiographical Novel.* NDP725.
Classics Revisited. NDP621.
More Classics Revisited. NDP668.
Flower Wreath Hill. NDP724.
100 Poems from the Chinese. NDP192.
100 Poems from the Japanese.† NDP147.
Selected Poems. NDP581.
Women Poets of China. NDP528.
Women Poets of Japan. NDP527.
Rainer Maria Rilke, *Poems from The Book of Hours.*
NDP408.
Possibility of Being. (Poems). NDP436.
Where Silence Reigns. (Prose). NDP464.
Arthur Rimbaud. *Illuminations.*† NDP56.
Season in Hell & Drunken Boat.† NDP97.
Jerome Rothenberg, *Khurbn.* NDP679.
Seedings & Other Poems. NDP828.
Nayantara Sahgal, *Rich Like Us.* NDP665.
Ihara Saikaku, *The Life of an Amorous Woman.*
NDP270.

St. John of the Cross, *Poems.*† NDP341.
W. Saroyan, *Fresno Stories.* NDP793.
Jean-Paul Sartre, *Nausea.* NDP82.
The Wall (Intimacy). NDP272.
P. D. Scott, *Crossing Borders.* NDP796.
Listening to the Candle. NDP747.
Delmore Schwartz, *Selected Poems.* NDP241.
In Dreams Begin Responsibilities. NDP454.
W. G. Sebald, *The Emigrants.* NDP853.
Hasan Shah, *The Dancing Girl.* NDP777.
C. H. Sisson, *Selected Poems.* NDP826.
Stevie Smith, *Collected Poems.* NDP562.
Novel on Yellow Paper. NDP778.
A Very Pleasant Evening. NDP804.
Gary Snyder, *The Back Country.* NDP249.
Turtle Island. NDP381.
Gustaf Sobin, *Breaths' Burials.* NDP781.
Muriel Spark, *The Comforters.* NDP796.
The Driver's Seat. NDP786.
The Public Image. NDP767.
Enid Starkie, *Rimbaud.* NDP254.
Stendhal, *Three Italian Chronicles.* NDP704.
Antonio Tabucchi, *Pereira Declares.* NDP848.
Nathaniel Tarn, *Lyrics . . . Bride of God.* NDP391.
Dylan Thomas, *Adventures in Skin Trade.* NDP183.
A Child's Christmas in Wales. NDP812.
Collected Poems 1934–1952. NDP316.
Collected Stories. NDP626.
Portrait of the Artist as a Young Dog. NDP51.
Quite Early One Morning. NDP90.
Under Milk Wood. NDP73.
Tian Wen: *A Chinese Book of Origins.* NDP624.
Uwe Timm, *Invention of Curried Sausage.*
NDP854.
Charles Tomlinson, *Selected Poems.* NDP855.
Lionel Trilling, *E. M. Forster.* NDP189.
Tu Fu, *Selected Poems.* NDP675.
N. Tucci, *The Rain Came Last.* NDP688.
Paul Valéry, *Selected Writings.*† NDP184.
Elio Vittorini, *A Vittorini Omnibus.* NDP366.
Rosmarie Waldrop, *A Key into the Language of America.*
NDP798.
Robert Penn Warren, *At Heaven's Gate.* NDP588.
Eliot Weinberger, *Outside Stories.* NDP751.
Nathanael West, *Miss Lonelyhearts & Day of the Locust.*
NDP125.
J. Wheelwright, *Collected Poems.* NDP544.
Tennessee Williams, *Baby Doll.* NDP714.
Cat on a Hot Tin Roof. NDP398.
Collected Stories. NDP784.
The Glass Menagerie. NDP218.
Hard Candy. NDP225.
A Lovely Sunday for Creve Coeur. NDP497.
The Roman Spring of Mrs. Stone. NDP770.
Something Cloudy, Something Clear. NDP829.
A Streetcar Named Desire. NDP501.
Sweet Bird of Youth. NDP409.
Twenty-Seven Wagons Full of Cotton. NDP217.
Vieux Carre. NDP482.
William Carlos Williams, *Asphodel.* NDP794.
The Autobiography. NDP223.
Collected Poems: Vol. I. NDP730.
Collected Poems: Vol. II. NDP731.
The Collected Stories. NDP817.
The Doctor Stories. NDP585.
Imaginations. NDP329.
In The American Grain. NDP53.
Paterson. Complete. NDP806.
Pictures from Brueghel. NDP118.
Selected Poems (new ed.). NDP602.
Wisdom Books:
St. Francis. NDP477; *Taoists.* NDP509;
Wisdom of the Desert. NDP295.
Yūko Tsushima, *The Shooting Gallery.* NDP486.